£5.00

D0318642

Best walks in North Wales

By the same author for Constable

A Cambrian Way
A guide to the Cleveland Way
A guide to the Cotswold Way
Holding the Heights

Best walks in North Wales

Richard Sale

Constable London

First published in Great Britain 1988
by Constable & Company Limited
3 The Lanchesters, 162 Fulham Palace Road
London W6 9ER
Copyright © 1988 by Richard Sale
Reprinted 1992, 1994
Set in Times 9 pt by
Rowland Phototypesetting Limited
Bury St Edmunds, Suffolk
Printed in Great Britain by
The Bath Press Ltd, Avon

British Library CIP data
Sale, Richard, *1946* –
Best walks in North Wales.
1. North Wales – Walkers' guides
I. Title
914.29′104858

ISBN 0 09 468250 X

For my parents

Contents

Illustrations

Illustrations

(*Photographs taken by Richard Sale*)

Maps

Acknowledgements

I would like to thank the staff of the National Library of Wales, Aberystwyth for their considerable assistance during the research for parts of this book.

I would like to thank Christine and Tony Oliver for their hospitality during the completion of the routes.

I thank Mike Rogers and Nathan Sale who accompanied me on some of my outings, and Susan Shorland for having assisted with the route mapping.

I thank Bob, Martin and Paul of Bristol and West Photography for all of their help, and both Tony Oliver and Mike Rogers for permission to use a couple of their photographs.

All photographs in this book were taken with Pentax camera equipment.

Introduction

In considering any book that advertises itself as including the 'best' of anything it is advisable to be certain of the criteria used in selection.

The three dozen routes that are included in this book have been selected to explore the variation of scenery that North Wales has to offer, from sea cliff and dune, through wooded valley and conifer forest, to bare, sometimes rocky, mountain, and to include some of the most attractive features on offer, from waterfall to mountain lake.

The routes do not, therefore, concentrate on high mountains, though there are several such high routes. Neither do they seek out 'unspoilt' countryside. One walk follows a Bronze Age route to finish near a nuclear power station: an extreme example illustrating the way in which some of the walks have been chosen to explore the history of man in the area, from neolithic times to the Celts whose heritage is still the Welsh birthright, from Welsh princes to the industries that exploited the mineral wealth of North Wales.

Most of the routes are circular. Exceptions exist only where to have 'bent' a route would have been to affect its character. In those (few) cases, suggestions for the use of public transport are made. A section at the end of the book deals with public transport for those who wish to reduce their need to find places to park, for although an attempt has been made to start walks near good parking facilities, the car-parks of North Wales can suffer from overfilling early in the day, especially on weekend days in summer.

The routes are concentrated in the Snowdonia National Park and that is as it should be – the National Park boundary was drawn, after all, so as to define the scenically excellent. However, as those who go often to Snowdonia know, the area has one of the highest rainfalls in Britain. Not for nothing are the waterfalls magnificent! Therefore, in order to offer wet-day alternatives – the mountains attract the rain, and frequently when it is very wet and miserable in Snowdonia, it is fine or, at least, acceptable away from the hills – some routes are offered in the 'rain shadow' regions: north, on Anglesey; west, on the Lleyn peninsula; and east, on the Berwyns and Clwydians. Advantage is taken of this decision to explore some excellent areas that are too often overlooked by the visitor intent on Snowdonia.

Finally, while every effort has been made to produce comprehensive and intelligible descriptions, and to back these up with equally clear maps, it must be emphasised that these should not be seen as anything but a supplement to possession of the maps mentioned at the start of each walk. Should you go off route, for whatever reason, only possession of the correct map will assist you back on to the correct line, or back to your transport.

STRUCTURE OF THE BOOK

Because the area covered by the book is a large one, the walks have not been grouped together by category (see below for a definition of the walk categories), but by area or hill range. To help with a choice of route in the appropriate category, all the walks are given at the end of this section in increasing order of difficulty, i.e. the easiest first, the most difficult last.

Each of the areas or hill ranges is dealt with in a separate chapter, and the introduction to each chapter deals with the particular historical, geographical or geological aspects of the area. By reading all of these introductions the reader is, therefore, able not only to build up, say, an overall history of North Wales, but to relate that history to the walks in an area.

The walks have been divided into three categories, Easy, Intermediate and Difficult, the divisions making allowance not only for the time that a walk takes, but also for the terrain it crosses, and for the amount, and severity, of any climbing it involves. In broad terms, an Easy walk will take about two hours, an Intermediate walk up to twice as long, a good half-day's outing, while a Difficult walk will take more than about four hours and will, for most people, be a long half-day's, or day's, outing. As will be seen from the table of walks at the end of this section there are also a handful of walks that lie on the border between Easy and Intermediate. These are walks that cover easy ground, but take rather longer than other

Easy walks without really warranting the higher classification.

The time given to each walk has been calculated using Naismith's Formula, a well-known walking aid, which allows one hour for each 5 map-kilometres (3 map-miles) covered by an unladen walker and adds half an hour for each 300 m (1000 ft) of ascent. For most people this formula will *under-estimate* the time taken on a walk, and the under-estimation will increase as the time given for a walk increases. The reasons for this are several: firstly, no one will complete a walk in route-march style, but will pause occasionally to admire the view or watch the wildlife, and no allowance for these stops has been made; secondly, the formula makes no allowance for the roughness or otherwise of the terrain or for the effects of the weather; thirdly, no allowance has been made for rest stops, and these may be both more frequent and longer on the longer walks; and finally, the formula assumes that the walker can maintain his level of performance indefinitely. While some people can maintain 'Naismith' walking for many hours at a stretch, many, especially those new to mountain walking, tire quickly and find not only that their rest stops increase and become longer but that they cover less ground while they are actually moving.

It is imperative, therefore, that the reader should use the walk-times as a guide only, and that newcomers to the area or to the sport should attempt lower-graded walks initially, and compare their actual performance with the given walk-time in order to gauge how long the more difficult walks will take them.

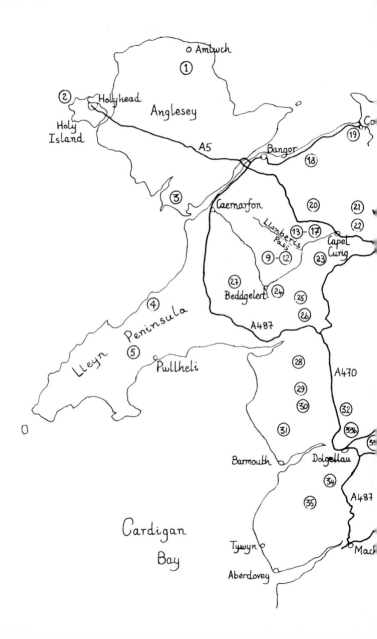

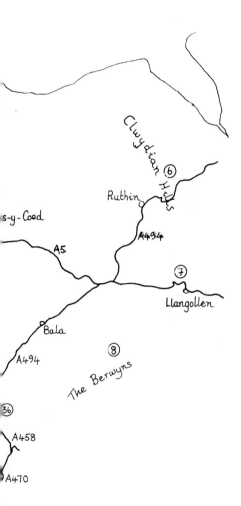

Clwydian Hills

⑥

Ruthin

s-y-Coed

A5

A494

⑦

Llangollen

Bala

A494

⑧

The Berwyns

㊱

A458

A470

h

THE WALKS

Name/Area/Number	Length in miles	Ascent in feet	Time in hours	Terrain and special difficulties
EASY				
Torrent Walk, Dolgellau (33a)	1½	375	¾	Distinct path, some steps.
Mynydd Bodafon, Anglesey (1)	2	300	1	Paths, but occasionally rough.
Cwm Idwal, Glyders (14)	2¾	300	1	Distinct path, occasionally uneven.
Gwydr Forest, Carneddau (22)	3	260	1¼	Distinct paths and roads. Some steps.
Aber Falls, Carneddau (18)	3	500	1¼	Distinct path, occasionally uneven.
Precipice Walk, Dolgellau (33b)	3¾	165	1½	Distinct path, one exposed but safe section.
Carn Fadryn, Lleyn (5)	2	720	1¼	Paths, occasionally indistinct.
Newborough Warren, Anglesey (3)	6	level	2	Sand and paths, one section of tidal shore.
Holyhead Mountain, Anglesey (2)	5	500	2	Paths, occasionally rough. Section of cliff-top path.
Two Lakes, Carneddau (21)	5¾	500	2¼	Paths, occasionally rough.
Offa's Dyke, Clwydians (6)	5½	1300	2½	Paths.

Name/Area/Number	Length in miles	Ascent in feet	Time in hours	Terrain and special difficulties
EASY				
Cnicht, Siabod/Moelwynion (25)	3¾	1800	2¼	Paths, occasionally steep. Some scrambling.
Llyn Dinas and the Aberglaslyn Pass, Siabod/Moelwynion (24)	6	800	2½	Paths, occasionally rough and uneven.
EASY/INTERMEDIATE				
Miners' Track, Snowdon (10)	6¼	1000	2½	Distinct path, occasionally uneven.
Coed-y-Brenin Forest, Rhinogs (32)	7¼	650	2¾	Distinct paths.
Castell-y-Bere, Cadair Idris (35)	6¾	500	2½	Paths, occasionally indistinct and rough.
Cwm Glas, Snowdon (12)	3¾	1650	2½	Indistinct or no path. Rough, occasionally very rough.
INTERMEDIATE				
Conwy Mountain, Carneddau (19)	6¼	1150	2¾	Paths.
Cwm Bochlwyd and Cwm Tryfan, Glyders (16)	5	1500	2¾	Paths, occasionally rough and steep.
Cwm Cowarch, Arans (36)	4	1650	2¼	Path, occasionally indistinct or absent. Rough.

Name/Area/Number	Length in miles	Ascent in feet	Time in hours	Terrain and special difficulties
INTERMEDIATE				
Valle Crucis and Eglwyseg Mountain (7)	12½	1000	5	Paths.
Moel Siabod, Siabod/Moelwynion (23)	6¼	2450	3½	Paths, occasionally rough and steep.
Drovers' Road, Rhings (31)	9	1150	3¾	Paths, occasionally boggy.
The Moelwyns, Siabod/Moelwynion (26)	5¾	2500	3¾	Paths, occasionally indistinct and rough.
The Berwyns and Pistyll Rhaeadr, Berwyns (8)	7½	2150	4	Paths, occasionally indistinct or absent. Rough.
Bronze Age Road, Rhinogs (28)	11¼	660	4¼	Paths, occasionally indistinct. Rough. Occasionally boggy.
Yr Eifl, Lleyn (4)	9	1650	4½	Paths. One steep section.
DIFFICULT				
Roman Steps, Rhinogs (29)	5¾	1970	3	Paths, occasionally rough. One section pathless. Rough. (This route has two shorter variations.)
Y Garn and the Devil's Kitchen, Glyders (15)	5	2300	3	Paths, occasionally indistinct. Rough. Some steep sections.

Name/Area/Number	Length in miles	Ascent in feet	Time in hours	Terrain and special difficulties
DIFFICULT				
Cwm Cau, Cadair Idris (34)	6¼	3280	3¾	Paths, occasionally indistinct or absent. Rough with steep sections, some exposed.
Rhinog Fach and Y Llethr, Rhinogs (30)	7½	2620	4	Paths, occasionally rough and steep.
Nantlle Ridge, Moel Hebog (27)	7½	3100	4¾	Paths, occasionally rough and steep. Exposed sections.
Watkin Path, Snowdon (11)	9	3600	5	Paths, occasionally rough and loose on steep sections.
Cwm Dudodyn and The Northern Glyders, (17)	9½	3800	5¼	Paths, occasionally indistinct.
Tryfan and Bristly Ridge, Glyders (13)	6	3100	3¾	Paths, occasionally rough and steep. Considerable amount of scrambling, some exposed.
Horseshoe, Snowdon (9)	7½	3300	4½	Paths, occasionally steep and rough. Exposed scrambling in early stages.
Front Ridge, Carneddau (0)	12½	3300	6	Paths, occasionally rough. First climb steep and arduous.

THE WELSH LANGUAGE

The Celtic language that crossed to Britain from continental Europe split into two variants, the Goidelic language occurring in Ireland, Scotland and the Isle of Man, the Brythonic language in Wales and Cornwall. The two variants are now differentiated as 'Q Celtic' – Goidelic Celtic or Gaelic – and 'P Celtic' – Welsh, Cornish and the similar language of Brittany, Breton. The reason for the definition is in the pronounciation of 'qu'. Q Celtic pronounces this as 'c', while P Celtic pronounces it as 'p'. An easy illustration is the difference in the word for mountain. Welsh has *pen*, while Gaelic has *ceann*.

To the English eye the Welsh language is an unreadable mass of vowel-less words, consonants back-to-back. This impression is based on the misconception that the alphabets of the two languages are the same. In fact Welsh has extra consonants, 'dd', 'll' and 'ff' being letters – not as strange as it seems, for remember that English has 'w', i.e. uu – and can utilise 'w' and 'y' as vowels. While 'dd' and 'll' have their own sounds – the former as 'th'; the latter as 'thl' – 'ff' is pronounced 'f', the Welsh 'f' being pronounced 'v'. Thus Tryfan is pronounced 'Tryvaen' and *cwm* (a corrie or mountain hollow) is pronounced 'coom'. A second, and radical, departure from English is initial mutation, the alteration of the initial consonants of words when the final sound of the preceding word is of particular form. The reason for this appears to be straightforwardly aesthetic. However the (apparently random) interchangeability of, say, *fawr* and *mawr* (large) or *fach* and *bach* (small), not to mention other worse forms, e.g. *cam – gam – ngham – cham*, makes the casual observer wince.

Throughout the book the common form of place-names has been used, even when this has meant using an English version rather than the orthodox Welsh. Thus Anglesey and Lleyn are used in preference to Môn and Llyn, though Conwy and Caernarfon are preferred to Conway and Caernarvon. On the mountains it is common for Carneddau to be used rather than The Carnedds, though The Glyders is invariably used in preference to Glyderau.

An attempt at a comprehensive glossary of useful Welsh words is obviously doomed to failure, but the following is, I hope, a useful short list, to allow the walker to better understand the ground being traversed.

Aber, confluence, but usually a river mouth
Afon, river
Allt (Gallt), hill, especially if wooded
Bach (Fach, Bychan), small
Bedd, grave
Betws, chapel
Blaen, head of valley
Bont, bridge
Braich, arm
Bwlch, pass
Cadair, chair
Caer, fort
Capel, chapel
Carn (Carnedd), a pile of stones
Carreg, stone
Castell, castle
Cau, deep hollow
Cefn, ridge   celli – grove
Clogwyn, cliff
Coch (Goch), red
Coed, wood
Craig, crag
Crib, comb, narrow ridge
Cwm, mountain hollow, a valley with a backslope, as in the famous usage in Western Cwm below Everest
Dinas, town or hill-fort
Du (Ddu), black
Dwr, water
Dyffryn, valley
Eglwys, church
Eira, snow
Esgair, long ridge
Ffordd, road, pathway   FAEN – STONE

Ffynnon, well, spring
Glas (Las), blue-green
Gribin, jagged ridge   GROES – CROSS
Gwyn, white
Gwynt, wind
Hafod, summer dwelling, hillside house for summer use
Hen, old
Hendre, winter dwelling, valley house for winter use
Hir, long
Isaf, lowest
Llech, flat stone
Llethr, slope
Llithrig, slippery   LLWYN – GROVE
Llyn, lake
Maen, stone (*maen hir*, long stone or standing stone, i.e. menhir)
Mawr (Fawr), big
Moel (Foel), bare, rounded hill
Mynydd (Fynydd), mountain
Nant, stream, brook
Newydd, new
Ogof, cave
Pant, small hollow
Pen, peak
Pistyll, waterfall, usually a water spout
Pont (Bont), bridge
Porth, gate
Pwll, pool
Rhaeadr, waterfall
Rhyd, ford
Saeth, arrow
Sarn, causeway
Sych, dry
Tref, town
Twll, hole
Ty, house
Uchaf, highest
Waun, moor

Wen, white
Y(Yr), the, of the
Ynys, island
Ysgol, ladder

MAPS AND MAPPING

North Wales is covered by the following Ordnance Survey 1:50 000
Landranger Sheets:

    114 Anglesey (Môn)
    123 Lleyn Peninsula (Llŷn)
    115 Snowdon and surrounding area
    116 Denbigh and Colwyn Bay area (Dinbych a Bae Colwyn)
    124 Dolgellau and surrounding area (Dolgellau)
    125 Bala and Lake Vyrnwy and surrounding area (Y Bala a
         Llyn Efyrnwy)

The Snowdonia National Park is also covered by five 1:25 000
Outdoor Leisure Maps:

    16 Conwy Valley
    17 Snowdon
    18 Bala
    19 Harlech
    23 Cadair Idris/Dovey Forest

The majority of the walks in this book are covered by these larger
scale maps. For those that are not, the information on each walk
specifies the relevant 1:25 000 Pathfinder sheet that does cover it.

The maps given for each walk use conventional map signs, with
the addition of the following:

∞∞∞∞	intact wall		—o—o—	gate
o o o	broken wall		—⦷o—	kissing gate
+++++	fence or hedge		—≪—	ladder stile

—⌐— stile   — · — · — indistinct path

— — — distinct path   S   start point

· · · · ·   no path   ①   feature of interest

Each map has a scale bar. They are drawn from personal
observation, and so are not guaranteed to be absolutely to scale.
Every effort has been made to ensure accuracy, but from time to
time fences are erected or, more unusually, taken down. The author
would be grateful for any information on such changes so that the
book can be kept up to date.

MOUNTAIN SAFETY AND THE COUNTRY CODE

The area around Snowdon (Yr Wyddfa) receives an average of 4000
mm (160 ins) of rain annually, and most of the upland areas of the
National Park receive in excess of 2500 mm (100 ins) of rain.
Snowdonia is close to the sea, so the temperature decreases with
altitude more markedly than in other mountain areas. The norm is
for a drop of about 1°C every 150 m (about 2°F/500 ft), while on
Snowdon the drop can be as high as 1°C/100 m (2°F/300 ft). This
means that the temperature on the summit of Yr Wyddfa could be
as much as 8°C (15°F) lower than that at Pen-y-Pass. In addition,
the prevailing south-westerly wind can be quite strong, hitting
Snowdonia after an uninterrupted blow across the Irish Sea. The
effect of wind on exposed skin has recently received publicity in the
occasional publication of 'wind chill' temperatures. Wind increases
the convective heat loss from exposed skin, the wind chill
temperature being the still-air temperature that would be required
to produce the same heat loss, that is, to 'feel as cold'. If the skin is
wet, the chilling effect is further enhanced. It is not possible to give
a simple rule of thumb for wind chill, as the effect varies with air
temperature and wind-speed, but as an example a 25 km per hour
(15 m.p.h.) wind would reduce an air temperature of 10°C to an

apparent temperature of about 2°C. Thus, if you are enjoying a reasonable day at Pen-y-Pass, with a temperature around 20°C (68°F), the apparent temperature on Snowdon's summit in a fresh wind could be just above freezing.

These comments are not made to make the mountains seem a playground for supermen, or to dissuade anyone from walking on them. It is just that it would be irresponsible not to warn any newcomer to Snowdonia of the tricks it can play. Be prepared: if you have not done so already, get a copy of *Safety on Mountains*, a very small booklet from the British Mountaineering Council that tackles the very large subject of individual responsibility and safety.

It is also important that anyone contemplating expeditions into mountainous areas should be able to use a map and compass. If you are not familiar with these critical items, you could do no better than obtain a copy of Kevin Walker's *Mountain Navigation Techniques*, published in the same Constable series as this guide.

The majority of the walks in the book follow distinct paths. *Please keep to them.* The Park's only real pollution problem is people, and the cars that bring them. It is estimated that on a good summer's day there are as many as 1500 people walking to the top of Snowdon. On one occasion an estimated 1000 people, walkers and train riders, were congregated on the summit. Under that sort of traffic the laid pavements in towns would groan after a few months. So if on any of the walks the path is diverted to allow the ground to recover, or if there is a section of constructed pathway, be sympathetic to the Park wardens' problems. Of course it would be better if there were no obvious, scarring paths, but the only really successful method of reducing wear to zero would be to ban all walkers.

The Country Code
The Code was prepared by the Countryside Commission with the help and advice of the many organisations concerned with the welfare of the countryside.

Enjoy the country and respect its life and work.
Guard against all risk of fire.
Fasten all gates.
Keep dogs under close control.
Keep to public footpaths across all farmland.
Use gates and stiles to cross field boundaries.
Leave all livestock, machinery and crops alone.
Take your litter home.
Help to keep all water clean.
Protect wildlife, plants and trees.
Make no unnecessary noise.

Anglesey

During the last Ice Age, the south-flowing ice of what is now the Irish Sea met ice flowing down from the mountains of Snowdonia. Where the ice flows met they combined to form huge, abrasive sheets, one of which swept across Anglesey before turning southward across the Lleyn Peninsula towards Cardigan Bay, while another swept south along the line of the Dee estuary towards the Cheshire–Shropshire plain.

When the Ice Age ended, only a few thousand years ago, the meltwater filled some of the valleys that had been over-deepened by the passage of the ice sheet. One such valley or, rather, series of valleys filled to form the Menai Straits dividing Anglesey from mainland Wales. Another valley filled to divide Holy Island from mainland Anglesey. In each case the separation of the land masses is minimal: near Dyffryn (Valley), Holy Island is a mere 150 m away at high tide, while at Menai Bridge mainland Wales is perhaps twice as far. However, as armies have discovered throughout history, a channel 300 m wide is a very considerable obstacle, especially when, as is the case in the Menai Straits, the channel is scoured by a vicious current. Tide tables show a difference of about 1½ hours between the ends of the Straits, a difference that creates a current running, at its fastest, at about 8 knots. But though that makes the waters treacherous for man and his boats, it does not deter marine wildlife, and for its great diversity and interest the Straits were designated as one of Britain's first marine nature reserves. Those interested in the area's marine life, but lacking the experience to see it at first hand, should visit the Marine Zoo at Brynsiencyn – midway between Llanfair P.G. and Newborough – where there are well-stocked aquaria.

Beyond the Straits is Anglesey, and no one who visits can be left unaware that this is an historic island, or that it is Welsh. One route across the Straits is Telford's Menai Suspension Bridge, at the time of its construction (1825–6) one of the finest pieces of engineering in the world, being both long (nearly 600 ft) and high – Admiralty regulations required 100 ft of headroom from the high-tide point so that fighting ships could sail below. When the bridge was opened

the locals held a party at which the brave – and there were many –
ran across the suspension chains, 9 ins wide and, at their highest,
over 150 ft above the water. A cobbler mended shoes sitting astride
one chain at its mid-point, while a band played the National
Anthem on top of one tower and then, for good measure, repeated
the performance in mid-span having marched out on planks laid
across the chains.

A second route to the island takes the new Britannia bridge,
beneath which the main-line London to Holyhead and Ireland
railway runs. This bridge replaces the famous Stephenson tubular
bridge built in 1850 and, sadly, destroyed by a fire in 1970.

Beyond the new bridge is Llanfair P.G., a village with both
historical and Welsh connections, though the latter are more
accurately described as the linguistics of tourism rather than those of
'Cymreig'. On a column near the village stands a bronze statue of
the Marquis of Anglesey, cavalry commander and second-in-command
to Wellington at the Battle of Waterloo. The Marquis is famous for
his exchange with Wellington when, at the height of the battle, one
of his legs was blown off. Most stories have the exchange as: 'My
God, I've lost my leg.' 'My God, so you have,' but I must confess I
prefer the slightly more surreal and less frequently quoted
'My God, there goes me leg'. 'My God, so it does.'

The column, 91 ft high, was erected in 1816 to commemorate
both the Marquis, who lived at nearby Plas Newydd, and the battle,
though the statue, showing the noble lord resplendent with both
legs, was not added until 1860. The column can be climbed, the 115
steps repaying the effort of their ascent with excellent views over
island, straits and Snowdonia. As a digression, those interested in
statues of our warfaring heroes can visit one to Nelson placed near
the shoreline, behind the church. I am perplexed by the statue's
position – what did the Menai Straits ever do for Nelson, or vice
versa? – a perplexity apparently mirrored in Nelson's sculpted
features. Another admiral, Paget, was responsible for the likeness,
in 1873.

The linguistic claim to fame of the village is that of having the
longest place-name in Britain or most other countries, the famous
(infamous?) Llanfairpwllgwyngyllgogerychwyrndrobwllllantysilio-

gogoch, a name concocted in Victorian times to try to improve the
fortunes of the village when the railway line to Holyhead was
opened. Whether it was successful is debatable. Today the village's
real name, Llanfairpwllgwyngyll, is regularly *shortened*, to
Llanfairpwll, or Llanfair P.G.

In Welsh, Anglesey is Ynys Môn, the Island of Môn. Anglesey
almost certainly derives from Angles, the Germanic invaders who,
with the Saxons, pushed the original Celtic settlers of Britain back
to their mountain strongholds of Wales and Cornwall. Some see a
Scandinavian influence in the '-sey', though Saxon place names also
often end in '-ey'. Such is the academic conviction for this
derivation that it seems futile to challenge it, but I must confess to
never having been happy with a Saxon possession of the 'Mother of
Wales', and recall that the Celtic tribe that inhabited the island was
called the Deceangli.

The Welsh name Môn, immediately recognisable as being very
similar to Man, the next island to the north in the Irish Sea, is less
easily identified. Perhaps fancifully, it has been said to derive from
Mona, the upper circle of the Druids. Supporting this theory is the
fact that the island is known to have been a centre of Druidism, its
position as such being one of the reasons that the Romans felt it
imperative that it be invaded and destroyed. But the story of Môn
starts much earlier.

It is known that Anglesey was inhabited from neolithic times, that
is from around 4000 BC, because of the existence of the typical burial
chamber of that period. These chambers, called long barrows if the
earth that usually covered them is still intact, but having a variety of
names if 'naked', consist of a series of upright stones or slabs,
capped with a larger slab. In Cornwall such chambers are called
quoits, but the Welsh word, cromlech, is the more usual name.

One of the most interesting of these is close to our second walk,
for it lies just south of Holyhead, at 259 805. This chamber,
Trefignath, is a rare form of segmented tomb, a passageway about
12 m (40 ft) long being divided into three, perhaps, four segments.
Only two other examples of this type of tomb exist in England and
Wales, and these are both to be found on Anglesey. The tombs are,
however, relatively common in both Ulster and south-west Scotland

implying that in the third millennium BC there was interchange, perhaps trade, across the Irish Sea. More evidence for such interchange exists in the tomb of Barclodiad y Gawres at 329 708 between Walks 2 and 3. This tomb, the Giantess's Apronful, is magnificently and evocatively set some 15 m (50 ft) above the sea at the cliff edge, and consists of a narrow, slab-lined passage about 6 m (20 ft) long leading to a series of burial chambers. The whole is set in a circular earth mound 30 m (nearly 100 ft) in diameter. The Irish connection is found in the geometric patterns inscribed on five of the stones of the chambers – three where the passageway meets the chambers (two on the west and one on the east side), one at the back of the western, and one at the back of the eastern, chambers. The patterns, which look abstract but have been suggested to be, at least in part, stylised human forms, are very similar to those at New Grange near Dublin, and at other sites in Spain and Portugal. This suggest a possible sea-borne migration of New Stone Age peoples northward from Iberia.

Later neolithic tombs, the more commonly recognised cromlechs, also exist on Anglesey. Near Lligwy, and our first walk, is a curious chamber, at 501 860. Here a natural cleft in the rock has been utilised as a burial chamber, a huge 25-ton capstone being supported above the cleft by a series of small upright stones. The most famous chamber, however, is Bryn Celli Ddu, the Mound of the Black Grove, near Llanfair P.G. off the road towards Brynsiencyn and Newborough. This tomb lies at the centre of a stone circle whose construction preceded it. Little now remains of the circle and one school of academic thought has the builders of the tomb destroying its stones rather than using the site for its holiness. However, within the chamber there is an upright stone, a reminder of the power of the megalith in the minds of the builders. For the rest, the tomb – both chamber and surrounding mound – is almost complete; it is justly famous and well worth seeing.

The neolithic settlement of Anglesey suggests that the coastal plain was preferred, though it is possible that fewer sites remain in the centre of the island because of its more intensive usage over the succeeding centuries. Such few Bronze Age remains as still exist also lie predominantly on the coastal plain. One that should not be missed lies close to Walk 2, at 227 809. There stand two huge stones, each about 10 ft high, and about the same distance apart. These menhirs – that name is itself Welsh, from *maen hir*, long stone – are, in one sense, no great attraction; they are, after all, only a couple of old, upright rocks. But they are so evocative: in the right conditions of setting sun and wind-torn silence it is easy to understand the appeal of Earth Magic.

When the Iron Age came to Britain it was brought by people who, though belonging to several distinct tribes and coming, in all probability, from several distinct places, are grouped under the heading of Celts. No other race has such a strong link with Wales and the Welsh, as we shall see.

Of these Celtic peoples the most spectacular remains, here as elsewhere, are the hill-forts, the best of which we shall visit on Walk 2. On that walk we shall also pass a fine collection of huts from the same period. The most intriguing find however has now left the island, and its source lies beneath the runway of RAF Valley on the main island opposite the southern tip of Holy Island. Llyn Cerrig Bach, a small lake, was dredged before filling in 1943 when the runway was constructed to assist the war effort, and from it was removed a horde of Iron Age weapons and armour. The consensus of opinion is that the horde accumulated over a lengthy time, and that it represents votive offerings, probably as part of Druidic rites.

Mention of the Druids conjures up, in most minds, visions of men in flowing white robes and equally flowing and white beards, chanting ancient rites as the midsummer sun rises at Stonehenge. The reality is that Stonehenge pre-dates the Druids by many centuries and present-day Druids are the product of the over-imaginative mind of a curious Victorian Welshman. Of the real Druids almost nothing is known: the Celtic peoples of whom they were the priesthood left no written record, and those that did record them, the Romans, were the enemies of both people and priests alike and, therefore, very unlikely to be complimentary.

All that is known for certain is that the Druids were the Celtic priests, that they carried out certain rites within sacred oak groves, that mistletoe – romantically, cut with a golden sickle, which is nonsense because a golden sickle would be too soft for the job – was a magical symbol to them, and that they probably divined the future and placated their deities with animal or human sacrifice. The last point is disputed, especially with respect to human sacrifice, by the romantics who point out, correctly, that the Roman record is likely to be exaggerated and written specifically to cast the Druids in a bad light. The Romans were far too clever not to realise that total domination or integration of the Celts was only likely if their priesthood, who had a vested interest in fomenting disquiet, was forever silenced, their gods replaced with a more orderly collection. Julius Caesar's description of a huge wicker manikin stuffed with victims and set alight is strange – propaganda does not usually go to such imaginative lengths – but it is almost certainly true that some blood and entrails were spilled. It was, after all, only a matter of a couple of centuries since the now-civilised Romans had been doing the same.

Most learned opinion now sees Anglesey as a centre for Druidism. Its position, an island off the mainland Celtic lands, suited the people's 'other world' folklore, and it is likely that young men came here to be initiated into the sacred rites. It was inevitable, therefore, that the Romans would also come, to eradicate the sect. Following the real invasion of Britain in AD 43 – Julius Caesar's invasion of 55 BC had been little more than an investigative foray – and a steady advance across the country, an invasion of Anglesey was planned in AD 61.

The Romans were led by Suetonius Paulinus, who had constructed a number of boats for his infantry, his cavalry swimming their horses across. What they met, we read in Tacitus, was a sight at which they were 'gripped by fear':

> The enemy army was ranged along the shore like a forest of weapons and soldiers among which women ran ceaselessly about like Furies, shrieking imprecations, with black robes and dishevelled hair and torches in their hands. All around stood Druids with their hands raised to the sky howling wild curses.

But the Roman soldiers were professionals and they soon recovered their composure, survived the curses poured down on them, and routed the thronging mass. Then they cut down the sacred groves,

destroying the roots of Druidism. On the mainland this act of
desecration, as the Celts saw it, was a major factor in the rebellion
of Boudicca, an uprising which required the re-taking of Anglesey
by Agricola, this time almost bloodlessly, in AD 78.

Of the Roman remains on Anglesey the best are of the Caer Gybi
fort at Holyhead, near Walk 2, though the hill-fort we pass on that
walk also shows evidence of Roman occupation.

Following the departure of the Romans, Anglesey was briefly
taken by Irish Celts, themselves driven out by Celts from
Strathclyde under the, possibly legendary, command of Cunedda
who conquered and preserved the first recognisable kingdom of
Gwynedd. A later king, Catamanus, is remembered in an inscribed
stone now set into the chancel wall of Llangadwaladr – at 383 693 –
which runs *Catamanus rex sapientissimus opinatissimus omnium
regum* (Catamanus wisest and most renowned of all kings (lies
here?)). The stone was probably erected by the king's grandson,
Cadwaladr, after whom the village is named.

Around the time, and, perhaps, a generation before the time,
that the stone was being carved two decisive battles were fought, at
Dyrham, near Bath, and near Chester. The battles had their roots
in the inter-tribal warfare that was so much a part of the Celtic way
of life, and was to prove so disastrous in later attempts to keep
Wales free of English domination. To assist in one war Vortigern,
founder of the Kingdom of Powys, but now cast in the role of
betrayer of Britain, brought in Saxon mercenaries, fell in love with
the Saxon leader's daughter and gave Kent to the newcomers in
payment for her hand. That was in the mid-fifth century, and over
the next century the Saxons had gradually moved westward and
northward, pushing the Celts back. Occasionally they were slowed,
at one stage beaten to a many-decade standstill, perhaps by Arthur,
but they were a patient and relentless foe. By the end of the sixth
century they had reached the Severn, and the battle at Dyrham cut
off the Celts of south-west England – later pushed still further west
until they remained only in Cornwall – from those of Wales and
northern England. Then, in the early seventh century, the battle at
Chester completed the isolation of the Celts of Wales.

Following their isolation, the Celts continued to fight amongst

themselves, the major kingdoms, Gwynedd and Powys, arising in
the north. Gwynedd was to become crucial in Welsh history,
because its rulers held Anglesey, which became known as Môn
Mam Cymru, Anglesey, Mother of Wales. The reason for this was
simple: mainland North Wales was a rugged land, a narrow coastal
plain bordered by huge mountains whose presence produced, from
a farming point of view, a miserable climate. Anglesey was flat and
fertile; it was the granary of the kingdom. The Menai Straits, the
wide rings of the Snowdonian peaks, the outer moat of the Conwy
river and the foul weather were defences better than any human
castle builder could have designed or built. Throughout the history
of the struggle for independence, these defences, and fertile
Anglesey, were crucial to Welsh resistance. When Edward I made
his Ring of Stone to hold the Welsh princes in check he built a castle
to hold the river crossing at Conwy, one to hold the Menai Straits,
at Caernarfon, and one to hold Anglesey, at Beaumaris. Gwynedd's
royal court was at Aberffraw, near our third walk, though those
who visit the village today can be easily forgiven for finding it
scarcely credible that Llywelyn the Great used it as his base while
securing a principality that was as united and independent as Wales
had become in the Middle Ages. Typically, on his death his work
was undone by his warring sons. From here too, the final prince of
the royal line of Gwynedd, Llywelyn the Last, rode out to
ignominious death.

Walk 1   Mynydd Bodafon

Bodafon is one of a number of small hills that rise above the flat
plateau that is Anglesey. The rocks that underlie Anglesey are some
of the oldest in Britain, but the scenery of the inland area of the
island, though pleasant and pleasantly empty, is a little
monotonous. That monotony is broken up by the isolated hills of
which Bodafon is one of the better examples, both in height and
form. Technically these hills are monadnocks, a name deriving from
a peak in the Appalachians whose geology was studied early. A
monadnock is an erosion survivor, that is a remnant of rock that has
resisted the forces of erosion because of its hardness. Bodafon is a

Walk 1: Mynydd Bodafon

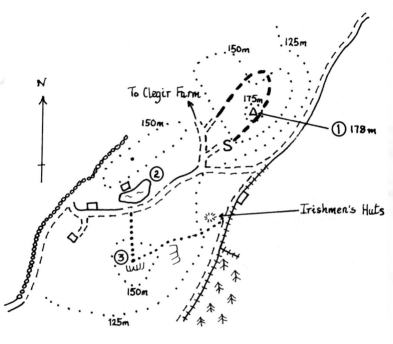

150m   125m

To Clegir Farm

150m

175m

① 178m

S

②

Irishmen's Huts

③

150m

125m

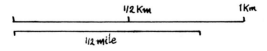

1/2 Km   1Km

1/2 mile

remnant of some of the hardest rocks of the Mona complex, as the sheet of very old, pre-Cambrian rocks that lies across northern Anglesey is known. Its vegetation is also markedly different from that of the surrounding land. There can be seen the gently rolling, green fieldscape typical of the island's centre, while here there are the jagged rocks, low gorse and heather scrub more reminiscent of 'real' mountains.

Walk category: Easy (1 hour).

Length: 3–4 km (about 2 miles).

Ascent: 90 m (300 ft).

Maps: Landranger Sheet 114; Pathfinder Sheet SH48/58 (Red Wharf Bay).

Starting and finishing point: Car-park at 471 852, signed for 'Clegir Farm', reached by a minor road that leaves the A5025 Benllech–Amlwch road at Brynrefail (481 869).

From the car-park the highest point of Mynydd Bodafon, at 178 m (583 ft) and suitably marked with an Ordnance Survey triangulation pillar, can be comfortably reached by any of several paths that wind up through the heather and gorse. At the right time of year the vegetation is delightful and offers a marked contrast to the softer scenery below. From the triangulation pillar the views to the north, east and west are spectacular (see (1) First viewpoint). Beyond the summit pillar the hill continues northward, and walks of any short distance can be made along the paths among the heather. Return to the car-park and follow the minor unfenced road away from the true summit of Bodafon passing a lake to the right (see (2) Mountain tarn). Beyond the lake go left and over wilder country to reach the outcropping rocks that break through the heather cover on this southern end of the hill. From the highest outcrop (care is needed on these – there are occasional vertical drops which, though short, can take the unwary by surprise), the view southward to the

Snowdonian peaks is the finest of those ranges to be had anywhere
in Wales (see (3) Second viewpoint). From the highest outcrop the
paths among the heather or, rather, the lack of them makes route
descriptions futile, but go eastwards, that is towards the sea, to find,
as the lichen- and moss-covered slabs finish, a large circle of
bracken that marks a series of now barely discernible Cytiau'r
Gwyddelod or Irishmen's Huts which are explained in note (1) of
Walk 2 below. From here return to the car-park by path and road.

(1) *First viewpoint (472 854)*

From the summit of Mynydd Bodafon the eye is drawn, at first, to
Parys Mountain, unmistakable with its contorted landscape below a
conical tower. It is known that both the Celts and the Romans
mined copper from the hill, but it was not until the last third of the
eighteenth century that anyone made a serious attempt to discover
how good the copper veins of Mynydd Parys might be. The answer
to the question was that they were astonishingly good, and for the
last quarter of the century the hill was both the largest and the
richest copper mine in Europe, yielding around 3000 tons of high
grade ore annually. The ore was both mined and excavated, the two
companies working the hill cutting a pair of huge pits, one many
hundreds of feet deep. By the early years of the nineteenth century
ore production was falling, the rich copper vein that ran near the
surface having been all but exhausted, but the importation of a
Cornish manager with deep mine experience revived the hill's
fortunes and it enjoyed another 25 years of staggeringly high
production. By 1830, however, fortunes were on the wane, though
attempts to earn a living from the hill continued until the early years
of this century. It is now over 80 years since the hill echoed to the
sound of blasting. The effect on the area around the hill and around
Amlwch where the ore was smelted prior to shipping was, by all
contemporary accounts, devastating. Fumes and run-off from
settling tanks on the hill – where run-off water was held to extract
the last ounce of metal – killed off crops and vegetation for many
miles around. With the cessation of activities the landscape around
the hill recovered, but the hill itself did not and, indeed, may never
recover.

At one stage I considered offering Mynydd Parys as a Best Walk, but though fascinating for its industrial archaeology – the conical tower is the base of a windmill – and for the fantastic variety of colours in the rock and in the debris cones, the hill is hardly aesthetically pleasing, a discordant array of rubbish ancient and modern, and is a potentially lethal mix of unstable rock and old mine shafts – no place for unattended youngsters.

On a handful of occasions each year some who go to Mynydd Bodafon are treated to a sight so magical that it would be easy to believe in the Celtic 'other world'. Late in the evening, as the sun is setting on a day especially clear, so probably after continuous rain, Ireland's Mountains of Mourne rise from the Irish Sea to stand in silhouette against the sun. On such days the visitor is also usually treated to a view of the Isle of Man and the Lake District.

To the east of Bodafon is Moelfre and a length of jagged coast that has torn the bottom out of many a ship. None is more famous than the *Royal Charter* wrecked there in 1859 in the teeth of a storm of such unimaginable fury that it is still spoken of in awe. In all, this storm, on 25 October, sank 133 ships off Britain's coast killing over 800 people, half of them on the *Royal Charter*. The ship is famous not only for this huge loss of life, but for the gold she was reputedly carrying, many of her passengers being Liverpudlian men returning from work in the Australian gold mines. Officially she was carrying around a third of a million pounds' worth of gold – at 1859 prices! – much of which was salvaged, but the value of the passengers' personal property was never known and has excited imaginations ever since. Only in 1985 did anyone make a serious attempt to salvage the rest of the ship's gold and the finds were amazing.

Several centuries before the wreck of the *Royal Charter*, Moelfre was the scene of another great loss of life, this time at the hands of men. Henry II sent a fleet to the north coast of Wales to re-supply his land campaign, but the ships entered Moelfre Bay, soldiers coming ashore to pillage the neighbourhood. A contemporary Welsh account of a later outcome of this landing, when some of Henry's men were killed, recalls the great era of the Celtic bards

Mynydd Bodafon

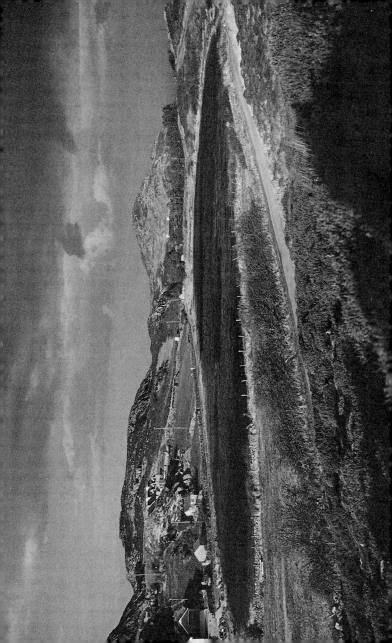

singing the praises of their warrior chiefs. It talks of the local hero, Owein, 'the prince who does not grovel', who attacked the invaders, putting them to the sword so that around Moelfre were 'a thousand war cries, slaughter on flashing slaughter, spears upon spears, terror on raging terror, drowning upon drowning, and the Menai's ebb blocked by the flooding streams of gore and dyed with the blood of men in the sea . . . and dying men in heaps before the red-speared king'.

More peacefully, the view west extends over Llyn Alaw, Anglesey's largest body of water, to Holyhead Mountain, and takes in the distinctly modern silhouette of Wylfa nuclear power station, the youngest and largest of Britain's first generation, Magnox, stations. Near the station, the village of Llanbadrig is named for St Patrick, Ireland's patron saint, who is reputed to have sailed from the village on his mission to the Emerald Isle.

(2) *Mountain tarn*

This small sheet of water is a tarn rather than a pond, and is one of two near the base of Mynydd Bodafon. The tarn is a near-perfect example of a rock-basin lake, water being held in a basin of impervious rock carved out by the glacial ice of the last Ice Age. Most glacially formed lakes are formed either behind dams of glacially-borne terminal moraine, or as long 'finger' lakes in over-deepened valleys, so these rock-basin lakes are interesting geography lessons.

(3) *Second viewpoint*

Though all of the features visible from the first viewpoint can be seen from here, what dominate the view and inevitably draw the eye are the Snowdonian peaks. In the walk description I maintained that this was the finest of all views of the range, and I make no apologies for so bold a claim. From left to right, as the Carneddau rise from Conwy, give way to the Glyders, then Snowdon, the Nantlle ridge and on down the Lleyn peninsula as the Rivals fall into the sea, the mountain blocks of northern Snowdonia are lined

Snowdonia from Mynydd Bodafon, with Pen-yr-ole-wen on the extreme left, then Tryfan, Bristly Ridge, the Glyders, Elidir Fawr, the Llanberis Pass, and the Snowdon group

up, the passes of Llanberis and the Ogwen valley being clearly
delineated.

Walk 2   Holyhead Mountain and Gogarth Bay

The summit of Holyhead Mountain on Holy Island is the highest
point on Anglesey, some idea of the dimensions of what was, before
the re-drawing of country boundaries, Wales's lowest lying county
being seen in the fact that about half of the mountain's 220 m
(722 ft) exist as sea cliff rising from Gogarth Bay.

The whole bay area, in and on the water, on the cliffs, on the
cliff-top common and in the air, is alive with wildlife, which is dealt
with in note (8) to the walk.

Walk category: Easy (2 hours).

Length: 8 km (5 miles).

Ascent: 150 m (500 ft).

Maps: Landranger Sheet 114; Pathfinder Sheet SH28/38 (Holyhead
Caer Gybi).

Starting and finishing point: Car-park at 210 818 near the end of the
minor road from Holyhead to South Stack and the lighthouse.

From the car-park go back to the minor road. Across the road and
over a stile a path is reached that leads to a fine archaeological site
(see (1) Cytiau'r Gwyddelod). Our route now goes along the road
(left from the car-park, right from the huts), taking the path to the
right after the café to the left. This path meets a metalled road that
is followed towards the radio station (see (2) Radio station). Before
this is reached go right along a track towards Holyhead Mountain.
When steps are reached, take a narrow path to the right, to the
summit. From the summit the view is spectacular (see (3) First
Viewpoint). Descend on a path that heads towards the Holyhead
breakwater to the obvious ramparts of Caer-y-Twr (see (4)
Caer-y-Twr).

Just beyond the wall, go left at a junction of paths and left again when a more distinct path is reached. At any convenient point leave this path to cross rough ground to a path beside which run overhead lines taking power to the North Stack signal station. Do not go to the station however, but straight on when a path to it leaves rightwards to reach a notch in the cliff with fine views of the Stack (see (5) North Stack). From the viewpoint an indistinct, but fairly obvious path leads back to steps at the foot of the climb to Holyhead Mountain. Along the way there are fine views of the Gogarth cliffs that rise, in places, 80 m (260 ft) from the sea, representing one of the finest rock climbing areas in Wales(see (6) Rock climbing).

Beyond the radio station go right to reach a path that is followed to the top of the steps to South Stack lighthouse (see (7) South Stack). The steps are beyond an archway, and here the walker has a choice – to descend the 403 steps to South Stack base, the only way back up being by way of the same steps, or to go left to a break in the lane wall, right, from where a track that skirts the edge of an impressive drop is followed to Ellen's Tower, the RSPB's observation tower (see (8) Ellen's Tower).

From the tower a path at the cliff edge, or one that goes more directly across the cliff-top common, leads back to the car-park.

(1) *Cytiau'r Gwyddelod*

In 1865 it was recorded that on this site there were the remains of about 50 huts, though today only about twenty remain, fourteen on the Welsh (Cadw) site and a further half-dozen in the fields to the north-east. Those that no longer remain were destroyed by thoughtless farming. The huts are Celtic, i.e. Iron Age, in origin and are almost certainly associated with the fort, used as a refuge, on the summit of Holyhead Mountain. The circular huts would have had a conical roof, supported by a central wooden upright. In several of them there are, now barely visible, remains of hearths, and upright stone slabs that presumably mark the position of beds and benches. Some of the huts are rectangular rather than circular, and finds in these suggest they were workrooms.

The name means 'Irishmen's Huts', from a legend that they were

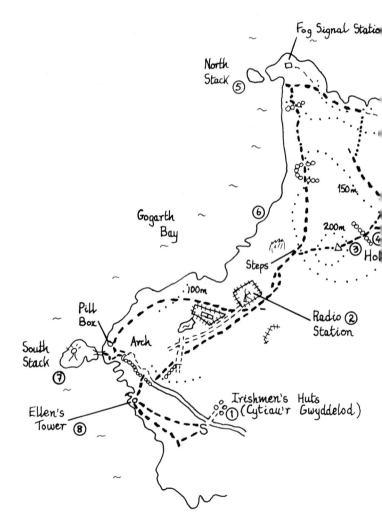

Fog Signal Statio

North
Stack ⑤

Gogarth
Bay

⑥

150 m

200 m ④

△ ③

Hol

Steps

100 m

Radio ②
Station

Pill
Box

Arch

South
Stack

⑦

Irishmen's Huts
○○ ① (Cytiau'r Gwyddelod)

Ellen's
Tower ⑧

S

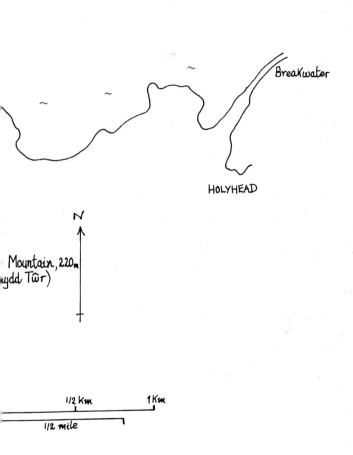

Breakwater

HOLYHEAD

N

Mountain, 220m
(ydd Tŵr)

1/2 Km   1 Km

1/2 mile

occupied by refugee Goidel Celts fleeing the invasion of Ireland by
Brythonic Celts, though there is no archaeological evidence to
support this folk memory.

(2) *Radio station*

This serves as a Post Office radio link with the Isle of Man.

(3) *First viewpoint*

Those blessed with perfect viewing conditions may see either, or
both, the Wicklow Mountains or the Mountains of Mourne in
Ireland, each range being about 75 miles away. Also visible are the
Isle of Man and the Snowdonian peaks. The Lleyn peninsula, the
hills of Yr Eifl beautifully laid out, is seen all along its length, with
Bardsey, Isle of Saints, off its tip. The nearer view is dominated by
Holyhead, Anglesey's principal town. In Welsh the town is Caer
Gybi, that name deriving, in part, from a fort built beside a
sheltered inlet by the Romans as part of the defensive system
against Irish raiders. The remains of the fort – and they are quite
extensive, three of the four corner towers remaining and the walls
still standing to 4½ m (15 ft) – circle the church of St Cybi, a saint
who provides the town with the rest of its name. The harbour's
breakwater, about 2½ km (1¾ m) long, is the longest in Britain,
and its presence is the reason for the huge quarry scar on our
mountain's north-eastern side, vast quantities of rock having gone
into the construction. The other side of the town's harbour is, in
part, a natural spit of land, Salt Island, so named because salt was
extracted from seawater there in the seventeenth century. At the
landward side of the island is an arch commemorating a stay – a
reluctant stay, the weather was too bad for sailing – in the town by
George IV in 1821. The arch also represents the start (or finish) of
the A5 that ends (starts) at Marble Arch, London, the road thus
having the oft-quoted privilege of being the only British road that
begins and ends at a triumphal arch!

(4) *Caer-y-Twr*

The summit of Holyhead Mountain was a hill-fort in Celtic times,
but here instead of the normal bank-and-ditch fortification a
dry-stone wall served as a defensive barrier on the side away from

Radio masts and Holyhead Mountain

the sea: the steep cliffs protected the seaward side. The wall
encloses an area of about 17 acres, enough to hold the inhabitants of
the hut village and, probably, several more villages of similar size.
In the north-east corner the entrance to the fort is still visible and in
places the walls, still about 3 m (10 ft) high, are topped by a rampart
walkway. The gap in the ramparts on the northern side has been
suggested to be a breach made during an attack. Ironically, in view
of the name given to the Irishmen's Huts, the most likely raiders
during the fort's period of use, the early centuries AD, were the
Irish. Near the summit there is evidence of a Roman-built
watchtower, itself almost certainly erected to watch for pirates.

(5) *North Stack*

The modern building here is a Fog Signal Station. On the hill
nearby, however, are the ruins of a much older signal station built in
1814 as one of a chain of eleven that signalled, by semaphore, to
Liverpool that the Irish packet boat, or a tea clipper, had been
sighted. The line-of-sight distance to Liverpool is about 80 miles,
and it was reckoned that message transmission took about one
minute. The signal was, of course, dependent on the weather and
the stations were rapidly replaced by telegraph as soon as it became
available.

The cliffs at this northern tip of Gogarth Bay are very
spectacular, rising almost vertically for nearly 100 m (330 ft) and
having had some huge caves gouged out of their softer rocks by the
action of the sea.

(6) *Rock climbing*

The cliffs of Craig Gogarth were probably the most important
centre for rock climbing in England and Wales during the 1960s
when the huge expanse of steep, unclimbed rock drew leading
climbers away from the mountain crags.

*By an agreement negotiated between the Nature Conservancy
Council and the British Mountaineering Council a ban on rock
climbing, to protect nesting birds, covers the area from just north of
the South Stack steps to Ellen's Tower for the period from 1 February
to the third week of July.*

Gogarth Bay and North Stack

(7) *South Stack*

The South Stack lighthouse was completed in 1809 and beams a single flash of light once every ten seconds across 20 miles of the Irish Sea. Those who are interested in the light and in the construction of the lighthouse can visit on every weekday afternoon unless there is fog. The trip to the lighthouse is worthwhile even if it is not visited, not least for the crossing of the little suspension bridge that takes the visitor from the mainland to the small knob of rock on which the lighthouse sits. In the right conditions of a running tide this crossing can be quite exciting. Considering the way the bridge is anchored at each end it comes as no surprise to discover that its construction was more complicated than that of the lighthouse: it was not finished until 1827. More complicated I can believe, but 18 years' work more complicated? How, I hear you ask, did the keepers reach the lighthouse in the intervening years? A rope was strung across the gap and they were hauled over in a wooden box slung below it! I rather imagine that work on the bridge did not begin in earnest until someone said, perhaps after a particularly harrowing trip, that enough was definitely enough.

As mentioned, there are 403 steps from cliff-top to bridge, but there is compensation on the journey, in either direction, from the occasional view into what the climbers call Mousetrap Zawn after a particularly famous and spectacular route. The climb winds its way up some really fantastic rock architecture. At this point the rocks of the Mona complex are bent, perhaps tortured would be a better description, into a series of folds. Since the original strata of the rock were a series of horizontal layers, the exact structure of the folds can be followed with ease. Not surprisingly the folds at South Stack are of considerable interest to the professional geologist as well as the amateur, and this has become one of the prime geological sites of Wales.

(8) *Ellen's Tower*

The tower was constructed in 1868 for Ellen, wife of Anglesey's MP at that time, W. Stanley, and it is the same Ellen who is remembered in the plaque – a modest little token! – on the tower wall. 'May all who visit this place bless her memory.' The tower, originally conceived as a summerhouse, is indeed a blessing for

those who visit the Gogarth cliffs to study the bird life, for it is now
an observatory for the RSPB. The society holds, on lease, a reserve
that includes Holyhead Mountain, the cliffs of Gogarth Bay
including South Stack, and the maritime heathland of Penrhos
Feilw Common about a mile to the south-east, a site that is also of
botanical interest. Nine species of sea-bird nest on the cliffs, the
members of the auk family being of particular interest. Few who
come to the reserve can fail to be enchanted by the puffin, in
appearance the clown of the bird world, with its astonishing landing
technique of helicoptering its wings and stepping out of the air on to
the cliff. The puffins breed on the earthy, lower cliffs, as they nest in
burrows. The sight of a puffin's multi-coloured bill appearing from a
dark hole in the grass frequently brings enthusiastic shouts in the
observatory. About 500 pairs of puffin breed at Gogarth, with about
the same number of razorbills and perhaps 2000 pairs of guillemot.
All the auks are recognisable by their fast, stiff-winged,
wave-hopping flight. I declare an interest, however, in the fulmar
which I suggest is the finest of all fliers and a joy to watch. Also
notable at the reserve are the choughs, elegant birds, their sleek
black plumage set off by red legs and beak. Usually there are five or
six pairs nesting at Gogarth, a sizeable fraction of Wales's breeding
stock. The birds will never be widespread, their very specific eating
habit – probing for insects – meaning that the winter mortality rate
will always be high. This eating habit contrasts strongly with that of
the other members of the crow family, several of which – raven,
carrion crow and jackdaw – are frequently seen at the reserve; they
tend to be opportunistic feeders and, hence, are on the increase.
The cliff-top heath is home to stonechats, linnets and whitethroats
and both common and cliffs are frequently quartered by peregrine
falcons as well as the more usual kestrels. The heath also provides
cover for passage warblers. Being a coastal site Gogarth is visited by
passage sea-birds and receives its share of blown-off-course rarities.
On a beautiful summer's day in 1987 the author missed, by 30
minutes, no less than four bee-eaters that had entertained a largish
crowd near Ellen's Tower, and, after watching newly fledged
choughs learning to fly, he left in good time to miss a black-browed
albatross!

The lucky visitor will see grey seals, which breed in the area, sunning themselves on the rocks at the base of the cliffs, or languidly floating in the calm waters of the bay apparently intrigued by climbers and visitors alike.

Walk 3   Newborough Warren

It would be difficult to find a greater contrast to the sheer cliffs of Gogarth Bay than Newborough Warren where a huge area, some 15 sq km (6 sq miles), is covered by sand dunes. From a conservation point of view, however, the areas are similar, each supporting quite different, but equally important, colonies of plants and animals. Newborough, as a village, has a (relatively) short history. When Edward I wanted to build a castle on Anglesey so that never again could it be Mam Cymru, the Mother of Wales, he chose a site that could be readily reached by sea near a beautiful piece of marshland, called, in consequence, in the courtly French of the time, Beau Marais. Unfortunately there was a village of local Welsh near the proposed site and, presumably fearing seditious intrigues, the king decided to move them. The chosen site for their 'New Borough' was a miserable, exposed spot near the bottom left-hand corner of the island. The villagers were reluctant to go, so Edward offered a financial incentive, not a bribe, but a fine to a few residents, including the local doctor, who were showing especial lethargy. The new villagers of Newborough, 'Welsh-ised' to Niwbwrch, found that the land to the west of their new home was fertile and enthusiastically cut the scrub cover, exposing both houses and new-won fields to the prevailing westerly winds and soon finding both inundated with sand. Marram grass was planted to stabilise the dunes and so important did it become to the villagers that a law was passed in the reign of Elizabeth I expressly forbidding anyone to cut it.

Walk category: Easy (2 hours).

Length: About 10 km (6 miles).

Ascent: Level ground.

Maps: Landranger Sheet 114; Pathfinder Sheet SH 36/46 (Caernarfon).

Starting and finishing point: Forestry car-park at 406 634 at the end of the road through the forestry plantation, signposted in Newborough village for 'Beach and Llanddwyn Island'. There is a charge for use of the car-park, which is not high for those intending to spend time, savouring the area to the full, but is not cheap if the visit is a flying one. It is possible to walk on forest tracks all the way from the village, but that does add several miles to the walk, and cannot be recommended at the expense of, say, a trip to Llanddwyn Island.

From the car-park take the path to the beach and go right to walk along the beach itself towards the now obvious Llanddwyn Island. To the right, as we walk, is a high bank of sand behind which is the forestry plantation. The beautifully sculpted sand, here and there burying a section of fencing, is delightful. To the left is the sea, and the tide-mark collection of shells, seaweed and flotsam. The shells are endlessly fascinating and a good collection of types can soon be made from the elegant razors to the gnarled oysters. The debris, most of it far from biodegradable, is a disgrace, but it must not be allowed to detract from the beauties of a frequently empty shore. Llanddwyn Island is an island for an hour or so around high tide, but the booted can wade and the patient can wait. The island is part of the Newborough Warren Nature Reserve and so it is important to keep to the track across it. The walker can and should go to the extreme tip of the island (see (1) Llanddwyn Island). Those who crossed on a rising tide may now have to wait for the water to recede. Retrace the outward journey to the dune gap for the car-park, but continue along the beach. As the forestry ends, the Warren proper begins, and it is necessary to take the first opportunity to reach it, although there are breaches in the wall of sand that soon hems in the walker on his left side (see (2) Newborough Warren). Occasionally I have tried, and watched

Walk 3: Newborough Warren

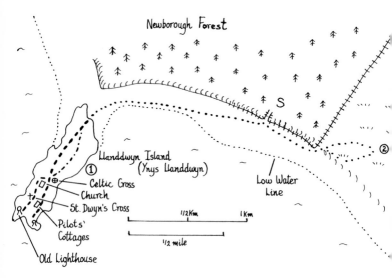

Newborough Forest

Llanddwyn Island
(Ynys Llanddwyn)

①

— Celtic Cross
— Church
St. Dwyn's Cross
Pilots'
Cottages

Old Lighthouse

S

Low Water
Line

②

½ Km   1 Km

½ mile

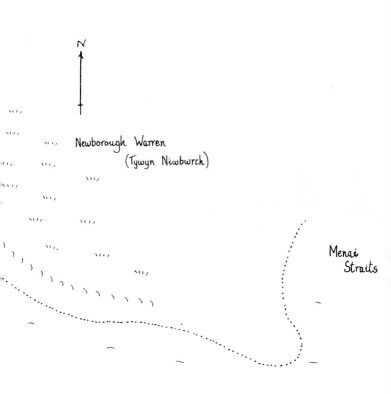

N

Newborough Warren
(Tywyn Niwbwrch)

Menai
Straits

others try, to scale the sand walls. It is possible with perseverance, and is relatively safe – but be careful of high, overhanging sand cliffs which could collapse, burying the climber. The victory over the dune wall is, in any case, pyrrhic, elation rapidly being replaced by irritation as sand is found in boots, pockets, nose . . .

In principal the walker can follow the narrowing beach all the way to Abermenai Point from where it is a mere kilometre (½ mile) to the coast a few kilometres along from Caernarfon, but it is probably better to wander among the dunes for a time, and the quoted mileage and time assume that this is what the walker will do. Return to the car-park is, again, by way of the beach.

(1) *Llanddwyn Island*

The rocks of the island are part of Anglesey's pre-Cambrian sub-strata, and so represent some of the oldest in Britain. That alone makes them fascinating – imagine, the rocks are at least 600 million years old – but in addition the coloration is excellent, the island, thrusting out into the sea, is beautifully positioned, and the distant peaks of Lleyn's Yr Eifl make a superb backdrop. Near the summit of the island are the remains of a medieval abbey church built on the site of a fifth-century hermit chapel of the Celtic saint, Dwyn. The abbey became rich, in a modest way, and was, in fact, the richest in the Snowdonian area when it suffered the same fate as all the religious houses in England and Wales – dissolution at the hands of Henry VIII. A contemporary engraving shows that the abbey, probably constructed in the early sixteenth century, was cruciform with a circular tower, but all that now remains are three of the chancel walls. The Celtic cross near the site is modern, erected to commemorate the discovery of human bones during excavations. The Latin cross commemorates the saint herself. St Dwyn came to this lonely spot, so one legend has it, to escape the memory of an unhappy love affair. Another version has her betrothed to a man she disliked and praying to God for salvation in the form of impotence for each of them. God provided a potion which worked on St Dwyn and turned her intended into a block of

Yr Eifl from Newborough beach

ice, although whether this is meant to be taken literally or is poetic licence for frigidity is not clear. Whatever the reason for her coming she could not have stayed without having some feeling for the beauty of the spot. In support of this, another legend says that as she lay dying she asked God to move a rock that was blocking her view of the sunset over Aberffraw, and God did so.

As one crossed in love St Dwyn was not surprisingly looked to for advice on matters matrimonial, although if the second legend is true she was far from the right choice. The well near the abbey ruins is said to hold a miraculous eel, placed there by the saint: if a lover sprinkles breadcrumbs on the well water and covers them with a handkerchief the eel will rise to eat the crumbs. If the handkerchief is undisturbed all will be well, but if it is disturbed the lover's partner will be unfaithful.

Astonishingly, Giraldus Cambrensis, the famed Gerald of Wales who toured the principality with Archbishop Baldwin in 1188 to drum up support for the Third Crusade, does not mention St Dwyn and her well. I say astonishingly because Gerald had a real ear for a miraculous tale, collecting them almost, it seems, as a hobby. One story he tells, not specifically related to Llanddwyn, but none the worse for that and not, in any case, related to any particular spot in Anglesey, is of a stone in the shape of a human thigh-bone that could not be permanently removed from its position. If carried away, even if thrown into the sea weighted with other rocks, it returned to its spot the following morning. It was also, Gerald claimed, a strong birth control agent; any union enacted near it would not produce a child, but, during the act, great beads of sweat ran off the stone!

Beyond the abbey remains, at the tip of the island, are a terrace of cottages, formerly the homes of local pilots, and a disused lighthouse. Off the tip are several small islands, one of the largest, and the furthest, being Ynys-y-cranc, the island of crabs.

(2) *Newborough Warren*

Newborough Warren is the sixth largest dune site in Britain, though half of it now lies under the forestry plantation – during the planting

Newborough Warren with the mountains of Snowdonia behind

of which the remains of some of the early sand-enveloped farms of
Edward I's new village were found. The half of the site that does not
lie beneath conifer is a National Nature Reserve both for its plant
and for its animal life. Chief among the plants is marram grass, an
elegant grass for all its occasional scrubby appearance, but there is
also sand couch and lyme-grass as well as other salt-hardy species.
As with all dunes there is an abundance of snails, with finely
coloured shells, so many in fact that the local herring gulls, here as
everywhere one of the most opportunistic of species, eat them in
quantity. Insects also thrive, particularly moths of which there are
many dune-specific types. Interestingly, as a walk in the dunes will
show, the habitat is not monotonous: there are wetter and drier
areas, shade and sun spots and each has its own microculture. In
addition to the herring gulls there are terns, great aerial performers,
and cormorants and shags nest on Llanddwyn Island. Rarer breeds
that might be seen by the very lucky visitor include the short-eared
owl and possibly the once regular Montagu's harrier.

The Lleyn peninsula

Geologically the Lleyn peninsula is a straightforward extension of the Snowdonian peaks, but it is obvious to even the most casual of observers that geographically it is quite different. The similarity lies in rock structure, with underlying beds of the sedimentary Ordovician strata through which various igneous rock masses have been thrust, forming the isolated peaks that rise steeply at various points along the peninsula. The difference is that here the igneous masses are lower, and that they were not accompanied by massive lava flows, so that there was no possibility of replicating the Snowdonian scenery. In addition, the lower height of the hard rock masses – Yr Eifl reaches 564 m (1850 ft), while the isolated Carn Fadryn reaches only 374 m (1225 ft), both low by Snowdonian standards – meant that during the Ice Age no glaciers formed on them, so that there was no carving of the cwms that are a distinctive feature of the angular Snowdonian ranges.

When the Ice Age was over the Lleyn was as we now see it. The sheet ice had reduced, though not totally eroded, the igneous masses and removed the limited lava flows that might have existed. It also deposited glacial debris, boulder clays, leaving a fertile land characterised by the monadnocks that were such a notable part of the views on Walks 2 and 3 in Anglesey. Monadnock, for those not familiar with the term, is explained in the introduction to the Anglesey section as being derived from a New England mountain, but it is also worth noting that more than one writer has pointed out the similarity the first part of the word bears to *mynydd*, the Welsh for mountain. Perhaps then, a Celtic word that found its way to America before finding its way back.

Interestingly the ice left the Lleyn looking exactly like a miniature version of Italy, leg and foot, even producing a (too small and misplaced) Sicilian island – Bardsey. Perhaps Nature has a particular interest in or liking for such shapes. The fertile land, coupled with the mild, if windy, climate that such sites close to sea enjoy, was an obvious attraction to settlers. There is still evidence of neolithic peoples on the Lleyn, especially on the coastal strip, although it is clear from a study of past records that considerable

numbers of sites, cromlechs particularly, have been destroyed,
either deliberately or as a result of agriculture. What remains is,
therefore, less spectacular than on Anglesey or, for instance, the
coastal strip west of the Rhinogs, but is no less interesting for that.
Perhaps the most interesting site is at 229 345 where a large
capstone is now supported on three uprights: originally there may
have been four. The extent to which sites such as this have been
integrated into the community can be seen from the local name of
Arthur's Quoit. The Celtic settlers, when they came, had no
explanation for these sites and, of course, no folk memory of their
erection, tending, as a result, to identify them with heroes or giants.
The valley of Nant Gwrtheyrn that we shall visit on Walk 4 also held
a neolithic tomb that was linked to a more recent man, although this
time real rather than legendary, and hated rather than revered. It
was said that to this valley Vortigern fled when the Saxons he had
invited to stay in Kent broke out westward, fleeing because his own
people, the Celts, realised both that a tiger had been unleashed and
that Vortigern's desire for the Saxon leader's daughter had been
responsible for the unleashing. The valley, still occasionally called
Vortigern's Valley, was secret and secure, if windswept and lonely,
and there he died. In the seventeenth century, romantics searching
for the last stronghold of the dead king excavated a mound which
they believed was his last castle. Their enthusiasm for the dig meant
that for excavation we must read destruction, and it seems likely
that they were, in fact, working on a large neolithic tomb – a long
barrow – although the description of their findings, the bones of a
man in a stone coffin, is strange since no such coffin burials exist at
neolithic sites. Perhaps, and most likely, having dug through the
earthy mound they found the inner cromlech, stone slab uprights
and capstone, mistaking it for a coffin. We are left to speculate since
nothing now remains.

The most important neolithic site on the Lleyn is at Mynydd Rhiw
(230 295), an isolated peak close to the glorious sand sweep of the
evocatively named Hell's Mouth. To the east of the hill there is a
fine tomb, at 238 288, but here it is the hill itself that is of
importance. In 1956 the burning of gorse on the hill stripped the
cover to reveal a series of hollows, each surrounded by a low bank

that was formed by the debris of the hollow's excavation. Further
work revealed more interesting features, including a quarry about
30 m (100 ft) long and 3 m (10 ft) deep, and assorted fragments of
the local rock, a particularly good material for the production of
sharp edges. It is now thought that the hill site was an axe factory,
axes, scrapers and knives being moved down to coastal sites near
Hell's Mouth for exporting. Radio-carbon dating shows that the site
was used from about 1200 BC right up to the coming of the Celts, a
period of about 1000 years.

A couple of miles north of Aberdaron one of Lleyn's isolated hills
dominates the countryside. This is Myndd Ystum, topped by the
hill-fort of Castell Odo. The hill-fort site is reckoned to be one of
the most important, archaeologically speaking, in Wales and is also
thought to be one of the earliest. The name Lleyn derives from the
same root as Leinster in Ireland, and it is believed that both Ireland
and this tip of Wales were colonised early as a wave of Celtic settlers
explored the Irish Sea from sites in northern France. This probably
occurred around the fourth century BC, and Mynyyd Ystum, an
obvious defensive position, is only a few miles from the sea whether
a landing was made at Lleyn's tip or on the north or south coast near
the tip. Excavation shows that there were several phases of
construction work on the hill, but only the initial phase was wholly
defensive, suggesting that there was no overriding need for defence
in this fertile peninsula. Even more evidence for this comes from
the last works on Castell Odo when, during the years of the Roman
occupation of Britain, the ramparts of the fort were deliberately
flattened and in some places hut circles were erected over the
rampart structure, suggesting that all need for defence had gone. It
appears that what Ptolemy's *Geography* calls Ganganorum
Promontorium, the Peninsula of the Gangani, was perhaps even
then – 2000 years ago – a peaceful farming community. The clue
might be in the name, for the Gangani were a tribe of Irish Celts
and this, with the relationship between the names Lleyn and
Leinster, suggests that the link between the Lleyn and Ireland was
strong and friendly so that the peninsula was not plagued by the
raids of which we saw evidence on Anglesey.

The Romans had important centres at Caernarfon (Segontium)

and at Tomen-y-Mur, near Trawsfynydd, one of the loneliest forts in Roman Britain, but no evidence exists for forts in the Lleyn, so it must be presumed that neither the locals nor the Irish caused them any great problems.

In addition to Castell Odo, there are other excellent Iron Age/Celtic sites, at Tre'r Ceiri and Carn Fadryn which we shall visit in Walk 4 and 5, and at Garn Boduan (at 312 395), now much afforested, but still showing evidence of ramparts and a very large number of huts. The name is believed to derive from Buan, a grandson of Llywarch Hen, and if that is true then the site could have been occupied as late as AD 600.

As a Celtic land, Lleyn had its share of saints. Indeed if the stories of Bardsey are true it had far more than its share! A famous one, St Beuno, is commemorated at Clynnog-fawr – at 415 495 – where the church bears his name. St Beuno arrived here from Welshpool having heard one day a Saxon calling his hunting dogs in, to Beuno, a foreign language. Beuno said, some say prophetically, that soon these men would invade the Celtic homelands and that it was therefore time to move west. If this really did happen near Welshpool, then Beuno had no need of prophecy, the Saxons already being about as far westward as they were going to reach. At Clynnog, Beuno was given land for a church and the stone across which this 'deed of gift' deal was struck is still in the church, its surface bearing an incised cross made, or so it is said, by the saint's thumb nail.

But talk of saints leads inevitably to talk of Bardsey. That name is believed to be Norse, deriving from Bardr, a Viking leader, the Welsh name being Ynys Enlli. The island was the site of Wales's first monastic house, founded in 622, though even then its religious use was ancient. It is said that St Deiniol was buried there in 584 and that the island had long been a place of spiritual retreat for Celtic Christians. Today little remains of the once famous St Mary's Abbey, whose land was supposed to hold the remains of 20 000 Celtic saints. In its day it was a place of pilgrimage, so difficult and dangerous to reach – the waters of Bardsey Sound are notoriously treacherous: the Welsh name, Ynys Enlli, means Island of Currents – that three pilgrimages to Bardsey were, on the scale of indulgences, the equal of a single pilgrimage to Rome. Gerald of Wales noted the island and, as one might expect, he found a miraculous story: those who dwelt on it did not die of disease, but of old age, so that everyone knew who would be the next to die – the oldest.

As the abbey of Bardsey flourished in Norman times it is no surprise to find, close to sites used for embarking for the island, fine Norman churches, even though such churches are not at all common in North Wales. In Aberdaron, St Hywyn's dates, in part, from the twelfth century and preserves a very fine Norman doorway. Here Gryffydd ap Rhys, King of Deheubarth, sought, and was granted, sanctuary when being pursued by followers of Henry I. At Llanengan, at the eastern end of Hell's Mouth, the church of St Engan has a superb square Norman tower in which are hung the bells from St Mary's, Bardsey.

Walk 4   Yr Eifl

The peaks on the northern coast of the Lleyn, so magnificent when seen from Anglesey, are called, in Welsh, the Prongs of the Fork, and it is not difficult to see why, there being three main peaks, neatly symmetrical and spaced. Sadly the beautiful name – pronounced Ear Ivel – has been Anglicised to Rival, hence Rivals, hence The Rivals, which is equally pleasant and even engimatic, since it is based upon a misconception, but wrong.

Though quite low, the peaks, composed, as we have seen, of hard, resistant rock, rise almost straight out of the sea, and, on the landward side, equally steeply from a low-lying plain. This position makes them seem high and, as we shall see, the open, windswept nature of the tops also gives them the feel of big mountains. Our route take us across each of the three fork prongs and visits a couple of evocative sites on the way.

Walk 4 : Yr Eifl

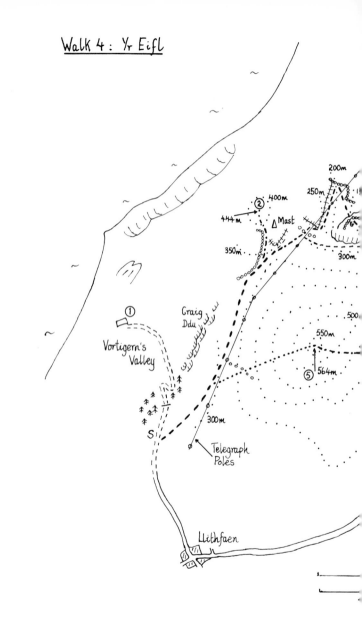

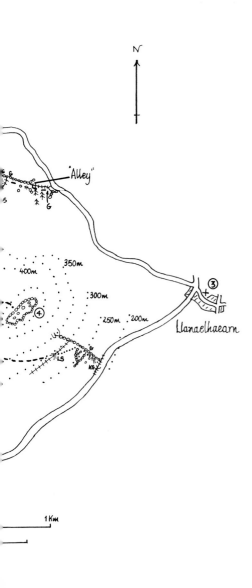

N

"Alley"

G

S
G

350m

400m

300m

4

250m 200m

3

Llanaelhaearn

LS

KG

1 Km

Walk category: Intermediate (4½ hours).

Length: 14 km (9 miles).

Ascent: 500 m (1650 ft).

Maps: Landranger Sheet 123; Pathfinder SH34/44 (Llanaelhaearn).

Starting and finishing point: The car-park at 353 440, reached along the minor road from Llithfaen on the B4417 Nefyn-Llanaelhaearn road. As the walk is circular and also passes through Llanaelhaearn and, if required, Llithfaen, either of those two villages can also be used as a base.

From the car-park take the metalled lane beyond the car barrier that leads down the tight valley (Vortigern's Valley) of the Nant Gwrtheyrn at least as far as the obvious elbow where there is a fine view of the old village, beautifully set where the valley meets the sea (see (1) Nant Gwrtheyrn) and of a waterfall down the cliffs of Craig Ddu, the Black Cliff. Return to the car-park and take the obvious track to the left (signed as a bridleway) that leads north-east across the flank of Yr Eifl. The track rises gently, offering an expanding view of Vortigern's Valley. At the base of the broken cliffs of Craig Ddu, at their northern end, there is evidence of an Iron Age settlement, with hut circles and a field system. The site is idyllic, though whether life also was, even in the summers of 2000 years ago, is a moot point.

When Bwlch yr Eifl is reach, *bwlch*, as you will by now have realised, being Welsh for pass, go left to the summit of the most northerly of Yr Eifl's prongs, keeping to the left of the signal repeater masts. (See (2) First viewpoint.) Return from the summit towards Bwlch yr Eifl, picking up a grassy track that leads downhill, with the power lines to the right, to the remains of a stone wall. From here the old line of the wall can be followed to a faint track that skirts along the top of a craggy outcrop before dropping down a steep gully in the outcrop line. This path is exposed at first and both steep and exposed in the gully, and should not be attempted by any but the experienced. An easier alternative is to continue downhill on the original track until another, more complete wall is reached. There go right, leaving the wall on a path through bracken to a gate in a wall close to a stream. Go through and follow the path left and downhill across the hill to reach the path coming down from the gully. A odd fence- and wall-bound alley is used to gain a path that leads to a small conifer stand which is traversed with a little difficulty – it is definitely easier for the very short – to a lane. Go right on the lane to Llanaelhaearn (see (3) Llanaelhaearn).

From the village follow the B4417, the 'upper road', towards Nefyn – an unfortunate piece of tarmac work, but the lane is quiet and safe. After about 1 km (1100 yds) there is a footpath sign (the second sign reached on the road from the village) to the right. Go over the stile and follow the field edge. An interesting ladder stile is reached – interesting because there is no fence or wall! – and other stiles are crossed, as the path rises up towards a pass between the main and southern peaks of Yr Eifl. Both should be visited, but for ease of returning to the start it is best to climb the main peak last. We therefore climb the southern peak (see (4) Tre'r Ceiri), followed by the main peak (see (5) Second viewpoint).

From the main Yr Eifl peak descend across rough ground to reach the pathway followed to Bwlch yr Eifl, returning along this to the car-park.

(1) *Nant Gwrtheyrn*

As mentioned in the introduction to this section, the valley of Nant Gwrtheyrn was known as Vortigern's Valley. One version of the legend of Vortigern and Merlin has the fabled castle of Dinas Emrys constructed in the valley, though it is generally accepted that the true position is near Llyn Dinas, as we shall see on Walk 24.

When Thomas Pennant, ever the intrepid, came here during his tour of Wales in the eighteenth century he described the valley as well as it has ever been described – 'Embosomed in a lofty mountain, on two sides bounded by stony steps on which no vegetables appear but the blasted heath and stunted gorse; the third side exhibits a most tremendous front of black precipice with the loftiest peak of the mountain Eifl soaring above; and the only

opening to this secluded spot is towards the sea, a northern aspect where that chilling wind exerts its fury.' At the far end of the valley, the old cottages belonged to quarrymen taking stone from Yr Eifl, but they were abandoned many years ago, allowing the curious to be alone with the ghosts of the past and the crash of the sea. Now, however, the cottages are again alive with voices, courses on the Welsh language being given here.

(2) *First viewpoint*

This spot has been claimed to have the finest views on the Lleyn and they are certainly magnificent, particularly to the sea, and out across it to Anglesey. The view towards the tip of Lleyn is also excellent. The quarries on the northern edge of the hill were for the extraction of Yr Eifl's hard, igneous core, a pale microgranite. The mineral deposits of the Lleyn were never as rich as elsewhere in North Wales, and though manganese, lead and zinc were worked, it was stone that was the major resource.

(3) *Llanaelhaearn*

This small, but pretty, village was almost certainly on the Saints' Road to Bardsey, the pilgrimage route. Several inscribed stones found in the vicinity, dating, perhaps, from as early as the sixth century, seem to verify this. So does the church, which dates in part from the twelfth century though it was much restored by the Victorians. It still retains a fine and ancient (sixteenth-century?) rood screen, and some well worked box pews.

(4) *Tre'r Ceiri*

No amount of words can prepare the interested visitor for the sight of Tre'r Ceiri on the southern prong of Yr Eifl. The name Tre'r Ceiri means Town of the Giants, and it is easy to see why it was chosen. The site is an oval, about 300 m (1000 ft) long and 100 m (330 ft) at its widest, and the retaining wall is about 4.5 m (15 ft) thick at its broadest. In places the wall still shows signs of a parapet walk. The wall is breached by two entrances, one on the north-western side, and one at the southernmost tip. Inside the wall have been found the remains of over 150 huts, mostly of the well-known circular pattern, but some that are egg-shaped.

The western prong of Yr Eifl beyond Vortigern's Valley

Presumably when in use the huts had a central pole to hold up a conical roof of bracken thatch. Other huts have been found outside the perimeter walls, on specially levelled platforms in the extensive scree cover of the hillside.

Though there have been excavations at the site, no very clear idea of the purpose of Tre'r Ceiri has emerged. It seems that there were two phases of occupation, one, pre-Roman, was of the simplest of the huts, but the second we know to have been during the Roman era, Roman pottery having been found in abundance. The village – surely this was more village than fort? – was, therefore, almost certainly inhabited until AD 400 though whether it was also inhabited before about AD 100 is less clear. No evidence has been found on the site for corn grinding, implying that the chief livelihood of the village folk was stock rearing, so what did they live on in winter? Was the village only inhabited in summer? If so, where did the people go in winter? Why were so many huts needed? It surely did not take this many people to look after the animals that Yr Eifl could support. Some people have suggested a purely defensive reason for Tre'r Ceiri's existence, but there is little evidence on Lleyn, as we have seen, for sea-borne raiders, and in any case protection from such hit-and-run raiders did not require elaborate huts. It just needed a wall – they would be gone by sunset.

Tre'r Ceiri is a mystery, and as with all good mysteries the odd legend has grown around it. Hence the name and, sadly, hence the destruction of the site. In the early nineteenth century an old woman in Llithfaen dreamed of a huge pot of gold buried in the ruins of Tre'r Ceiri. She talked of her dream, and within days the site had been wasted by avaricious villagers with pick and shovel.

One description I read of the village said it was more impressive than Stonehenge. In a technical sense – this much labour, these many tons of rock shifted – it may be, but it has nothing quite so mysterious or evocative. For all that, if you are alone, if the setting sun is dowsing itself in red steam out over the Irish Sea, and if the wind is moaning between the stones, Tre'r Ceiri has presence.

The highest prong of Yr Eifl beyond Tre'r Ceiri

(5) *Second viewpoint*
The highest Yr Eifl peak would be expected to have the best of the views, but the close high peaks to north and south do cut off some foreground. Nevertheless there are excellent views to the Snowdonian ranges, not as well delineated from here as from Anglesey's Mynydd Bodafon (Walk 1) but still very impressive.

Walk 5   Carn Fadryn

Of the isolated hills of southern Lleyn Carn Fadryn is the most impressive, an almost symmetrical cone, chopped flat near its top, and high enough to dominate the surrounding land.

Walk category: Easy (1¼ hours).

Length: 3 km (2 miles).

Ascent: 220 m (720 ft).

Maps: Landranger Sheet 123; Pathfinder Sheet 821 (SH13/23) (Nefyn and Tudweiliog).

Starting and finishing point: The village of Garnfadryn at 279 345 on the southern flank of the hill, reached from the B4415 that links the A497 Pwllheli-Nefyn road to the B4413 Llanbedrog-Aberdaron road.

From the village take the green lane that goes between the old chapel and the telephone box, continuing on to a gate when a farm lane goes off right. Beyond the gate is open hillside. Go left or right, following the wall to one of the paths that climbs to the lunar landscape at the top of the hill (see (1) Carn Fadryn). Return along the same lane to the village.

(1) *Carn Fadryn*
The conical hill of Carn Fadryn, formed of a granitic porphyry, is probably the remains of an ancient volcano, the lower hill to the

Walk 5 : Carn Fadryn

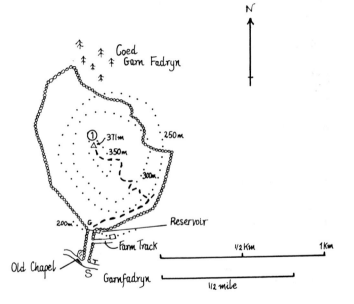

south east – Garn Bach at 285 345 – being formed from the remnants of a lava flow. The fortifications on the hill consist of two sets of ramparts, the inner, and presumably earlier, enclosing an area of 12 acres, the later enclosing closer to 25 acres. The remains of a Bronze Age cairn discovered on the site presumably pre-date both ramparts – which are assumed to be Iron Age, one pre-, and one post-Roman – and the cairn was levelled by the later builders. Much later a small castle was built on the peak's western extremity, a castle noted by Gerald of Wales when he came this way. It belonged, he said, to the sons of Owain.

Also on the site is a large flat slab of rock, known as Arthur's

Table, below which, legend has it, with shades of Tre'r Ceiri, there lies buried a pot of gold.

From the top of Carn Fadryn the views are dramatic. The peak lies almost exactly dead-centre in the peninsula, and commands the most extensive view of any site in the southern half of the Lleyn. The views to the sea coasts are excellent, the physical nature of the peninsula being shown to perfection, particularly the crescent of Hell's Mouth. The views of Yr Eifl and the Snowdonian ranges are equally fine.

Of the closer views, that eastward, towards the marsh land of Cors Geirch, centred at 313 363, is the most interesting. During the last Ice Age, ice covered the sea areas south and north of the Lleyn and, probably, also covered the peaks of Yr Eifl. In the central area of the peninsula however there was low-lying ice-free land in which glacial meltwater formed lakes if suitable hollows existed. One such lake, a large one and called by geologists Bodfean, formed to the east of Carn Fadryn. Llyn Bodfean had a limited lifetime: as the ice sheets melted the lake waters flowed out, chiefly southward towards Cardigan Bay. Several of the river and stream valleys in the area south of the bog owe elements of their present appearance, even of their present courses, to the previous existence of Bodfean, most notably the valley followed by both the Afon Horon – at one point under a bridge with the unlikely name of Inkerman – and the B4415. This valley actually took overflow water from the lake before the ice sheets melted, the water level in the lake having risen as a result of the inflow of glacial meltwater.

Carn Fadryn

The Berwyns and the Clwydians

To the east of the Snowdonia National Park are several upland
areas often neglected by the walker. The Denbighshire Moors –
now, pedantically, misnamed since the county boundary changes of
1974 erased the county of Denbigh from the map – lie immediately
to the east of the Park's eastern boundary which follows, very
roughly, the Afon Conwy to Pentrefoelas on the A5. It is as a series
of flattish, dullish hills to the north of the A5 between
Cerrigydrudion and Pentrefoelas that most people know the moors.

The lack of any volcanic activity in ages past, and the relatively
easy weathering of the Silurian strata, have given the moors a
uniform appearance that compares very unfavourably with the
angular peaks of most of the Park, or even with the less angular but
higher peaks of, say, the Carneddau. In addition, the poor drainage
of the area, a consequence in part of the monotonous landscape and
in part of the fact that the major effect of glaciation here was the
creation of boggy hollows, assists in producing an inhospitable
landscape. Indeed, so poor is the land that it has even been largely
shunned by the Welsh hill farmers who, as a race, seem more than
willing to try any piece of land that offers even a minimal chance of
success. Recently there has been extensive conifer planting on the
eastern tract of moorland – Clocaenog Forest – and the creation of
reservoirs – Llyn Brenig and Llyn Alwen – within the forest area,
and it is difficult to be unduly vociferous in opposition to that course
of action. The amenities that have followed in the wake of this
development, the visitors' centres, picnic sites, nature trails and so
on, may not be everyone's cup of tea, but given that somewhere had
to be sacrificed – and without addressing *whether* somewhere had to
be sacrificed – there were many places whose destruction would
have raised a far louder cry.

Those who love wild moorland country, with the occasional bout
of bog-hopping, should try the triangle of land bounded by the A543
Pentrefoelas-Denbigh road, to the east; the B5113 Llanrwst-
Pentrefoelas road, to the west; and civilisation to the north. There,
among the small lakes, such land is to be found in plenty, but it does
not, I suggest, offer one of the best walks in North Wales.

Technically the Denbighshire Moors are bounded to the east by the Vale of Clwyd, the broad, flat-bottomed and very fertile valley of the Afon Clwyd, though as the Vale is approached the moorland becomes lower and more amenable to farming so that real moor has disappeared long before the textbook boundary has been reached. Forming the eastern side of the Vale are the Clwydian Hills. As with the Denbighshire Moors, the Clwydians are formed from Silurian strata, and as with the moors they are relatively low – Moel Famau at 554 m (1820 ft) is little higher than Marial Gwyn at 519 m (1700 ft) – yet the hills are impressive, and worthy of attention. Why is this?

The answer is geographical as well as geological, a fault line having caused the eastern edge of the Vale of Clwyd to form a scarp slope, the rejuvenation of rivers draining the Silurian strata creating a marked effect on both the scenery – giving it the impression of a range of hillocks rather than a raised plateau as on the moors – and the drainage, which is here entirely adequate, allowing a more varied vegetation. In a couple of places the effect of rivers cutting back into the scarp has caused major passes through the hills. At Bodfari the line of the Afon Chwiler, the River Wheeler, is followed through the hills by the A541 Denbigh-Mold road, and was followed by the now dismantled railway. Further south the A494 Ruthin-Mold road traverses Bwlch-y-Parc.

The defensive advantages of the line of hillocks created along the spine of the Clwydians were not lost on the Celtic settlers of the Vale of Clwyd. Any one of the hillocks offers a panoramic view of the Vale, and a whole string of hill-forts lines the crest of the hillock ridge. Penycloddiau at 129 675 is oval, its ramparts – at one point the top of the rampart is still 12 m (40 ft) above the bottom of the ditch – enclosing around 40 acres. On Moel Arthur at 145 661 the conical hill has had a ditch dug to form a circular fort of around 10 acres. Moel y Goer at 149 618 is about the same size, but its defences are more elaborate with two, and at the northern end three, series of ramparts and ditches. Equally fine is the Foel Fenlli site at 161 600 that lies on Walk 6.

The defensive potential was also not missed by Offa, the king of the Mercian Saxons who achieved supremacy over the whole of

southern England in the last third of the eighth century and who
decided to construct a permanent border between himself and the
Celts of Wales. There is still controversy over whether the Dyke   ✳
that bears his name was dug to defend England from the Welsh, or
whether it was an agreed, negotiated border. Either way the Dyke
was constructed from the Wye to Llangollen clearly aiming for the
Clwydians, which providentially run north-south. With the hills as
part of the border, all Offa needed to do was to dig his way to the
sea near Prestatyn to have a complete, defendable rampart. The
work was never completed, Offa dying, as it is believed in AD 796. It
is thought that his death occurred in battle at Rhuddlan, the battle
being the result of attempts to establish a line for the last section of
Dyke. Such an occurrence, if true, seems to stretch the definition of
negotiation to ludicrous proportions.

South of Bwlch-y-Parc the Clwydians fall away into the valley
taken by the A5104 Bala-Chester road beyond which the scenery is
dominated by the magnificent limestone outcrops on the edge of
Eglwyseg Mountain, and by the valley of the River Dee.

The Dee, in Welsh Afon Dyfrdwy, is a beautiful river. Leaving
the tip of Bala's lake on a course steered between the mountain
blocks of the Berwyns and Migneint, it abruptly changes direction
near Corwen, flowing east and entering a high-sided, meandering
gorge from which it emerges beyond Llangollen. This gorge
represents a highly defendable valley separating the two sides of this
last mountain range between England and Wales. Indeed the line of
Offa's proposed border (as mentioned above, no work was
completed north of the Dee) goes very close to the gorge.

Defensive forts were built at each end of the gorge, at Castell
Dinas Bran, on Walk 7, and at Caer Drewyn at 088 444. Between
these two lies Glyndyfrdwy, home of a man with whom this area will
always be linked, Owain of Glyndyfrdwy, Owain Glyndŵr.

To understand the reasons behind the Glyndŵr – that spelling is
now the accepted Welsh, and is preferred to the Anglicised versions
Glendower etc, which retain neither the correct etymology nor the
correct pronunciation – rebellion it is necessary to understand the
politics of this area in the years between 1066 and 1400. When the
Normans reached the Welsh border they were not inclined to

✳ Offa's Dyke, I believe, is intended to prevent
cattle straying from England into Wales. RE '05

occupy and subdue Wales having, presumably, enough trouble with
the Saxons to keep them busy. Instead, along the border, or March
as they called it, they gave lands to the Marcher Lords whose duty it
was to prevent incursions of the Welsh into England. As
compensation the Marcher Lords were granted the right to increase
their lands by taking anything to the west which they felt able to
hold. This right, exercised frequently by the more warlike of the
lords, did nothing to improve relations between the two races and
led to prolonged, sometimes bloody, conflict, as we shall see later
when we return to Gwynedd. Finally, with laws enacted to reduce
Welsh rights and with their leaders killed, the Welsh fell into a
sullen peace.

In that peace men like Glyndŵr arose. Descended, if somewhat
tenuously, from the royal house of Powys, he was educated in
England, spoke French as they did at the English court, and fought
with courage and distinction for the English king. By 1400 he had
retired to his estates – the Dee gorge and another in the foothills of
the Berwyns – to enjoy his old age. It is not clear exactly how old he
was, but he could not have been less than 40 and was more likely 45.

A dispute with his neighbour, Lord Grey of Ruthin, a Marcher
Lord of the old school having little truck with 'barefoot Welsh
dogs', led to Grey being granted permission by Henry IV to take
Glyndŵr's lands, a grant that Grey took up with enthusiasm.
Warned of the attack, Glyndŵr went into hiding, where, probably
with reluctance on his part, he was proclaimed Prince of Wales and
started the rebellion. The first rebellious act took place in the Vale
of Clwyd, followers of the new Prince attacking the town of Ruthin
on 18 September 1400. In the following week this first army had
looted and set alight Denbigh, Flint, Hawarden, Holt and
Rhuddlan.

Though the rebellion was localised at first, it spread rapidly. The
castle at Conwy was taken and armed bands were soon at work all
over Wales. For seven years the war raged, each side breaking the
accepted rules of warfare by using scorched earth tactics, looting
monastic houses and killing civilians. Eventually the future Henry
V, a more resolute man than his father, and a better general,
brought an exhausted country and people to heel. Wales wanted

peace, almost at any price, and Glyndŵr, never captured, disappeared to die in secret. It is a point to ponder, when contemplating the beauties of the Dee gorge, that its ownership led to so much blood and suffering.

South of the Dee as it turns eastward towards Glyndŵr's gorge are the Berwyns, a small range of very fine hills. At first sight the hills seem a little tame to the walker used to Snowdonia's jagged edges, but that first sight is deceptive. The high peaks of the range lie above 800 m (2625 ft), high enough to have influenced ice movements. As a consequence the high ridge that links the main peaks has been hollowed out into cwms in many places, the cwms collecting water that is channelled eastward – the main Berwyn ridge lies north-south and is sculpted on its eastern side – towards the River Tanat. One, and strangely only one, cwm holds a corrie lake, that is a lake formed either in a rock hollow or, more usually, behind a morainic deposit, after the floor of the cwm has been over-deepened by moving ice – Llyn Lluncaws below Moel Sych. This cwm, with its rocky amphitheatre and well-set lake, is a fine place, and well worth the visit Walk 8 makes to it.

South of the high Berwyn peaks the Tanat valley impresses a structure on the landscape, but south-east of the valley and its tributaries, and north of the high peaks, the Berwyns are upland moor, featureless – except, now, for the increasing number of forestry stands – and occasionally boggy. This is land for the connoisseur, a harsh landscape, surprisingly open to the weather. In note (3) of Walk 8, a folk tale and a true story, each associated with the weather, are told.

South of the moorland that lies beyond the Tanat valley is Lake Vyrnwy, Llyn Efyrnwy in Welsh. The lake is a reservoir, created in the late nineteenth century by the building of a dam which required half a million tons of rock and 27 000 tons of cement. This dam, tiny by modern standards for all its impressive tonnage, holds back 13 million gallons of water used to supply Liverpool. The tree cover at the lake's shore was originally planted to increase rainfall (!) in the belief that conifers helped clouds form. Today they seem to increase the artificiality of the lake, though it has become a popular site with tourists and meets with the (guarded) approval of the RSPB.

To the east of reservoir, moorland and high ridge there is some
very civilised country, with a fine history linked to the Royal house
of Powys. Five miles east of Llanrhaeadr-ym-Mochnant is Sycharth,
at 205 258 but on private land, Owain Glyndŵr's preferred home,
now just a mound and the dry remains of a moat. Further south is
Mathrafal, at 128 116, now thought to have been the site of the
royal court of the princes of Powys. Much closer to the main upland
areas, Pennant Melangell, at 024 265, should be visited by anyone
with an interst in Celtic saint mythology and church architecture.
Here in 604 the Irish Virgin Saint, Melangell or Monacella,
confronted Brochfael Ysgithrog, Brochfael the Fanged, forced him
to call off his hunt for a hare that hid beneath her skirt and
impressed him so deeply that he gave her land for a church – though
he did not, apparently, give up hunting. The present hamlet church
is of great interest, and includes part of a twelfth-century shrine to
the saint.

Walk 6   Offa's Dyke on the Clwydian Hills

Our route includes one of the best sections of the Offa's Dyke
long-distance footpath, taking in a fine hill-fort, the highest point of
the Clwydians, and some very fine views into the Vale of Clwyd.

Walk category: Easy (2½ hours).

Length: 9 km (5½ miles).

Ascent: 400 m (1300 ft).

Maps: Landranger Sheet 116; Pathfinder Sheet 772 (SJ06/16)
(Denbigh (Dinbych)).

Starting and finishing point: The forestry car-park at 171 611 on the
minor road that leaves Llanbedr-Dyffryn-Clwyd at the first,
right-hand, bend of the A494, after the village church. The first
car-parks, at Bwlch Penbarras (160 605) near the cattle grid, can
also be used, as the route goes through them.

Walk 6: Offa's Dyke on the Clwydian Hills

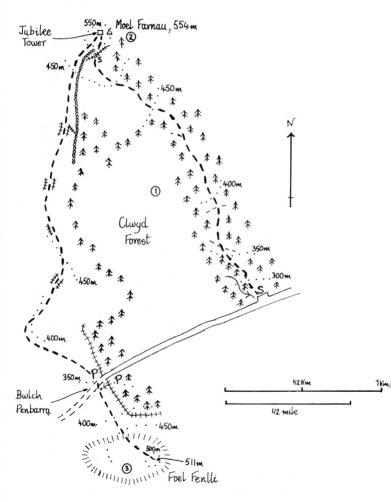

From the car-park follow the path beside the information board, rising steeply through the Clwyd Forest (see (1) Clwyd Forest) to emerge on the flank of Moel Famau. Take the obvious acorn-marked pathway to the summit (see (2) Moel Famau). From here, after the forest walking, it is difficult to resist the temptation to continue along the open ridge for a few hundred yards. The ascent of Moel Dywyll, the next peak on the ridge, adds about 3 km (2 miles) and 500 ft – taking about an hour – to our walk, and is well worth considering.

From the summit take the broad track that runs parallel to the forest edge all the way to the road at Bwlch Penbarras. Beyond, the climb to the Foel Fenlli hill-fort is equally well marked: keep to the edge of the forestry up through the heather to the top or follow the acorn-marked path (see (3) Foel Fenlli). To descend, go eastward, towards the Vale of Clwyd, then descend to a path that leads back to Bwlch Penbarras. Now go right, following the lane back to the car-park.

(1) *Clwyd Forest*
The forest near the car-park is mainly Japanese larch and the very attractive red oak. Further along the path the more usual mix of western red cedar, lodgepole pine and Sitka spruce takes over.
(2) *Moel Famau*
Moel Famau, the Mother Mountain, is the highest point on the Clwydian Hills, at 554 m (1818 ft), though this height must be taken to be slightly pessimistic, as the Ordnance Survey triangulation pillar is overtopped by many feet by the remains of the Jubilee Tower, a famous landmark on both sides of the hills. The tower was built in 1810, to commemorate the Golden Jubilee of George III. It was designed by a Chester architect called Harrison and in its original form consisted of a square base and a graceful spire. Sadly, in 1862 during a particularly violent storm, the spire was struck by lightning and its fall damaged the base. For a century the tower was then at the mercy of elements and vandals alike, and by 1970 was a considerable eyesore. In that year, European Conservation Year, it was repaired, and four fine, steel panoramic dials, made by apprentices of the Shotton Steel Works, were fixed to it. The dials

point out the places that can be seen from Moel Famau, and the distances to them. The view south, of the Llantisilio range, is especially good, though the eye is inevitably drawn westward to the peaks of Snowdonia – the Arans, Cadair Idris, the Arenigs and the ranges around Snowdon itself. To the east, Liverpool can be seen and on clear days the view north extends to the Isle of Man, the Lake District and Blackpool Tower. In the Clwyd Vale below stands the town of Ruthin, its castle, once that of Lord Grey, still visible.

(3) *Foel Fenlli*

Foel Fenlli, 511 m (1676 ft), is topped by arguably the most impressive of all the Clwydian hill-forts. It is an oval fort covering 24 acres and is protected by defences whose construction depends on the gradient of the hillside. All around the fort there is a single ditch and rampart with the rampart still rising to 3 m (10 ft) in places – in one place the distance from ditch bottom to rampart top still measures 10 m (33 ft). On the east side of the fort the hillside falls away more gently and two extra ditch and rampart pairs have been constructed. The fort had two entrances, in the south and west ramparts, and the turn of the wall, to make entry awkward for an invader and to expose his unshielded side to the defenders, can still be seen. Inside the fort the remains of about 35 hut circles have been identified. From the fort, looking north, in addition to Moel Famau, the hillocks topped by the forts of Moel Arthur and Penycloddiau can be seen.

Walk 7   Valle Crucis and Eglwyseg Mountain

The limestone escarpment of Eglwyseg Mountain represents one of the most impressive sights in the landscape of North Wales outside the Snowdonia National Park. Below the scarp cliffs is another fine sight, this time man-made, and also man-despoiled, the abbey of Valle Crucis. It is sad that the monastery is ruinous, but ruins are very picturesque and these lie in a beautiful position, the whole producing one of the loveliest sites in Wales. To the north of the

Jubilee Tower, Moel Famau

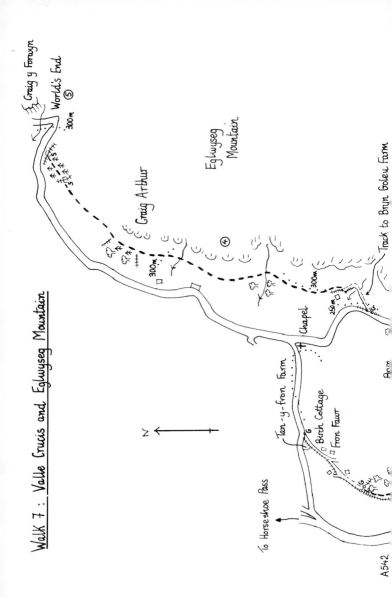

Walk 7 : Valle Crucis and Eglwyseg Mountain

Craig y Forwyn

World's End ⑤

300m

Craig Arthur

300m

Eglwyseg Mountain

Track to Bryn Goleu Farm

250m

Chapel

300m

Tan-y-fron Farm

Birch Cottage

Fron Fawr

N

To Horseshoe Pass

A542

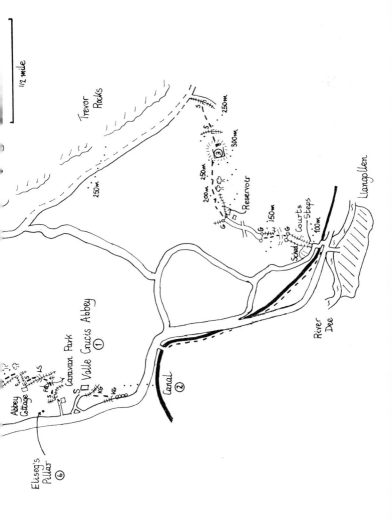

½ mile

Trevor Rocks

250m

250m

250m

S

S

300m

250m

200m

Reservoir

150m

100m

School
Courts
Steps

G

G

G

G

G

Llangollen

River Dee

Canal ②

Valle Crucis Abbey ①

Caravan Park

S

KG

KG

FB

ES

ES

ES

ES

Abbey Cottage

Eliseg's Pillar ⑥

abbey ruins is Eliseg's Pillar, an interesting historical object, while
to the south lies Castell Dinas Bran, an important hill-fort.

Nearby Llangollen has been a famous town for a great many
years. Its bridge over the Dee, a most elegant structure, dating from
the early twelfth century (during the widening of 1873 a stone was
found dated 1131), though widened in the mid-fourteenth century
and again in the late nineteenth, is listed as one of the Seven
Wonders of Wales in an old rhyme:

> Pistyll Rhaeadr and Wrexham Steeple,
> Snowdon's Mountain without the people,
> Overton yew trees, St Winefride's Wells,
> Llangollen bridge and Gresford bells.

In Walk 8 we visit Pistyll Rhaeadr and later we also visit Snowdon,
though whether we shall be lucky enough to have it to ourselves
remains to be seen.

Today Llangollen is more famous for its International
Eisteddfod, held annually in July, and for the white waters of the
Dee that form a course frequently used by international canoeists.

Walk category: Intermediate (5 hours).

Length: 20 km (12½ miles).

Ascent: 300 m (1000 ft).

Maps: Landranger Sheet 117; Pathfinder Sheet SJ24/34 (Llangollen
and Wrexham (Wrecsam) South).

Starting and finishing point: The car-parking for Valle Crucis Abbey
at 205 442 can be used, but this may not make you popular as it is
very limited. The only alternative, to use Llangollen itself, adds a
few hundred metres to the route, but does have the advantage of
involving a crossing of the famous bridge. If you do use the town,
cross the bridge, and turn right. Go left and up Wharf Hill, bearing
right over the canal bridge (Siambr Wen Bridge) to join the route
from Valle Crucis.

From Valle Crucis Abbey (see (1) Valle Crucis Abbey) go along the
road beside the abbey (and away from the caravans) and diagonally
across a field to a gate on to the main road. Go left and follow the
road around to the canal bridge. There go over the bridge (signed
'Motor Museum') to join the canal towpath (see (2) Shropshire
Union Canal). Follow the towpath to Siambr Wen Bridge using the
bridge to recross the canal. Now go across the road to gain steps and
a path beside the school, signposted for Castell Dinas Bran. This
path is followed easily across minor roads before reaching the open
hillside. Follow the track across the hill-fort (see (3) Castell Dinas
Bran) and down the far hillside to a stile. Go over this and
diagonally down and across the field beyond to a stile into a lane.
Turn left, and left again when another lane is reached.

Follow the lane (see (4) Eglwyseg Mountain) for about 2½ km
(1½ miles) to a signed track, right, for Bryn Goleu farm. The track
continues at the same contour level along the base of the crag to
World's End (see (5) World's End). Return by the same route to
Bryn-Goleu. Now go right along the lane, turning first left after the
Missionary Church of St Mary, hidden among conifers to the left.

Go down the lane until a lane to the left, signed 'No Through
Road, Footpath only', leads off. This is followed easily, through
fine woodland, to Abbey Cottage. Go left over a stile in front of the
cottage and follow the field edge, i.e. the hedge on your right. Soon
a ladder stile gives access to a small piece of woodland, a footbridge
and a lane to the main road. There go right to visit Eliseg's Pillar
(see (6) Eliseg's Pillar). From the Pillar return along the main road
to the abbey car-park.

(1) *Valle Crucis Abbey*
Valle Crucis means the Valley of the Cross, the cross in question
being Eliseg's Pillar which is described in note (6) below. The abbey
was endowed by Madoc ap Grufydd, Prince of Powys and a cousin
of Llywelyn the Great, around the year 1200, as a house for
Cistercian monks. The Cistercians were a new order, formed in the
early twelfth century and taking their name from the founding
abbey of Citeaux in France. The monks sought to re-establish a
simpler, harder-working version of monasticism. They refused

tithes and rents, wore poor clothes, had church vessels and ornaments made of wood or iron rather than gold as in some of the Benedictine monasteries, and were largely self-supporting. For their sites they chose 'unfashionable' spots, looking only for water, and caring little for the farming value of the land. The abbey remains of England and Wales that are in the country rather than the town tend to be Cistercian, and some magnificent sites they are: Rievaulx and Fountains, Tintern, Strata Florida and this one at Valle Crucis. When the monastery was dissolved by agents of Henry VIII the Abbot's Hall became a farmhouse, the roof of the church was stripped and gradually the whole became ruinous. Today the most impressive part of the ruin is what was the western wall of the church, with a huge window in early English style. The most complete part is the eastern end of the church and the chapter house beside it. Of the cloisters, the most easily recognised feature of a monastery for the layman, only the pathways and grass square remain.

The abbey is a delight, but the question must be asked why planning permission was ever granted for a caravan park beside it. It is enough to make you weep.

There is a story that Owain Glyndŵr was out walking early one morning, along the Dee banks from Glyndyfrdwy, when he met the abbot of Valle Crucis also taking the early morning air. Owain joked to the abbot that he was up very early but the abbot shook his head and said no, it was Owain who had risen very early, one hundred years too early. This story, prophesying the Tudor capture of the English crown, is probably a legend, but a very good one. Interestingly one version of Owain's last days places him here, and maintains that here, too, he is buried. If that is true it is a fitting resting place, and would also mean that he was close again to Iolo Goch, the bard who sang his praises throughout the rebellion and sang of his despair when it was over. Iolo Goch is certainly buried at Valle Crucis.

Valle Crucis Abbey

(2) *Shropshire Union Canal*

Strictly, the canal whose towpath we follow, the Llangollen Canal, is only a branch of the Shropshire Union, a waterway conceived in the Great Age of canals, around the turn of the nineteenth century, to join the great rivers, the Mersey, the Dee and the Severn. The Llangollen branch, completed in 1805, was built by Thomas Telford and links the Horseshoe Falls, constructed to keep the canal water-level correct, to the Shropshire Union near Ellesmere. On the way the canal crosses the aqueduct at Pont-Cysyllte, about 3 miles east of Llangollen, which can be seen from Castell Dinas Bran and is one of the most impressive pieces of canal engineering in Britain, and still navigable.

Pentrefelin, where we joined the towpath, was a quay, slate brought by tramway from the Horseshoe quarries being loaded there.

(3) *Castell Dinas Bran*

The castle, magnificently positioned on its conical hill, is an impressive place. But more than that, it is a place of magic and mystery. The Bran of the name was a mythical king of Britain whose sister, Branwen, was married to the king of Ireland. In an early Celtic story Bran gives the Irish king, as a wedding present, a magic cauldron which will restore life to the dead. Trouble comes, as it always does, and in the battle between the British and the Irish, the cauldron helps an Irish victory, maintaining the strength of the Irish army while the British army grows weaker. Finally Bran is wounded and is carried away to die. He makes his followers promise to bury his head on the White Hill in London which, after many adventures, they do. Bran has told them that as long as his head stays on the White Hill no invader from across the sea will defeat the British. Later, Arthur, envious of Bran's claim, digs up the head and, sure enough, after Arthur's death the Saxons defeat the British.

It is a good story, and there are two interesting details. Firstly the White Hill is thought to be Tower Hill, and since Bran also means crow, the head story has a direct counterpart in the tale of England

falling when the ravens leave the Tower. Secondly the name Bran is very close to Bron, who appears as a King in one of the 'Round Table' stories of the search for the Holy Grail. In the story there is a river like the Dee, and a castle of Bran on a conical hill above it. It seems probably that Castell Dinas Bran is thus one of the magical sites visited by Perceval, knight of the Round Table, in his search for the Grail, and should be as revered by followers of Earth Magic as is Glastonbury.

On a mundane level, the earliest fortifications on the hill are probably pre-Iron Age, but the castle is thirteenth-century, built by the same Madoc ap Grufydd who endowed Valle Crucis.

(4) Eglwyseg Mountain

The name derives from *eglwys*, Welsh for church, for this is the mountain above Valle Crucis. The limestone of the cliffs is Carboniferous, laid down about 400 million years ago and brought to the surface by the faulting that 'created' the Vale of Clwyd. Some idea of the colossal scale of such geological events can be gained by observing the position of the limestone scarp slope on the southern side of the Dee. It lies about 3 miles to the east.

At the base of the limestone cliffs there can occasionally be seen the remains of old lime kilns.

(5) World's End

World's End is the delightful name given to a small enclosed valley in a nick between the two cliffs of Craig-y-Forwyn, a popular three-tiered climbing crag, and Craig-yr-Adar. The name is an evocative one, and the spot is worth the visit just so that the visitor can say he has been there, but it is also an excellent viewpoint.

(6) Eliseg's Pillar

The pillar, which now stands to a height of about 2.5 m (8 ft) and is distinctly unprepossessing and even forlorn in its iron cage, is probably the most important Dark Age monument in Wales. Originally 3.7 m (12 ft) high and topped by a cross, the pillar was uprooted and vandalised during the Civil War by Puritan soldiers, the Puritans believing that all such devices were idolatrous at best, Papist at worst. When the pillar stump, all that now remains of the

The escarpment of Eglwyseg Mountain

original tall cross, was re-erected in 1779 the mound on which it stands was opened and found to contain the skeleton of a man, presumed to be Eliseg. Eliseg is mentioned by name on the stone, although the inscription is now almost illegible, as the reason for the pillar's erection. The cross was erected by Cyngen, who lists his antecedents in the inscription – which runs to 31 lines – making the pillar Wales's oldest surviving written pedigree. The best known part of the inscription reads: 'Cyngen, son of Cadell, Cadell son of Brochwel, Brochwel son of Eliseg, erected this stone to his great-grandfather Eliseg. It is Eliseg who united the inheritance of Powys, which had lain waste for nine years, from the power of the English, with fire and sword . . . Whoever shall read this hand-inscribed stone, let him give a blessing on the soul of Eliseg.'

Cyngen died in 854 during a pilgrimage to Rome and left no heir. His father Cadell, a contemporary of Offa, died in 808. The inscription therefore lists the line of Powys princes back about 200 years.

Walk 8 The Berwyns and Pistyll Rhaeadr

This route takes in some of the best of the scenery that the Berwyn range offers. Though it avoids the high moorland – which is, in any case, more of an acquired taste than a Best Walk – it does follow the high ridge, after starting in the very picturesque valley of a tributary of the Tanat.

Llanrhaeadr-ym-Mochnant, near the mouth of the blind valley we visit, was once the home of Dr William Morgan, famous for having translated the Bible into Welsh in the late sixteenth century. This action is thought to have been responsible for the survival of the language.

Walk category: Intermediate (4 hours).

Length: 12 km (7½ miles).

Ascent: 650 m (2150 ft).

Maps: Landranger Sheets SJ02/12 (Tanat Valley) and SJ03/13 (Llandrillo).

Starting and finishing point: The car-park at 074 295 below the waterfall of Pistyll Rhaeadr, reached along a no through road, signed from the village of Llanrhaeadr-ym-Mochant.

From the car-park go first to view the waterfall (see (1) Pistyll Rhaeadr), because that way you can see it again when you return. Now go back to the car-park and take a signed path through one gate to another. Beyond the second are a couple of trees that seem to be walking such is the exposure of their roots. The reason is that in very wet weather the path here is also a stream, and the earth has been washed away. Beyond another gate a signed, stepped path leads steeply off left. This is the return route. Going down rightwards is a raised green track leading to a stream, beyond which another obvious path rises up the valley side. This is the right of way, but there is a fence across the stream. It seems reasonable, therefore, to follow the obvious slaty path ahead to a junction of paths. Here go right down to the stream, ford it and go through the gate to a path going uphill. Where this path meets another, go sharp left on to a path heading off towards the Berwyns. Follow the path until it disappears, then follow the stream, the Nant y Llyn, back up to its mountain lake source, Llyn Lluncaws, mentioned in the general introduction to this section.

From the lake go up steeply to the col south of Moel Sych, going over that peak to Cadair Berwyn, from where the view along the high ridge to Cadair Bronwen (worth visiting if your time allows, as from it there is a fine view to the northern moorland of the Berwyns) is excellent. Now reclimb Moel Sych which was, before the redrawing of county boundaries, the highest peak in Montgomeryshire. From the summit do not go back along the scarp edge, but head south-south-west to pick up the stream that runs down the shallow Cwm Rhiwiau, the stream being a tributary of the Afon Disgynfa, the river that falls over Pistyll Rhaeadr. Just beyond the point where a smaller stream joins the Cwm Rhiwiau stream, on flat land to the west of the streams and half-hidden among the

Walk 8: The Berwyns and Pistyll Rhaedr

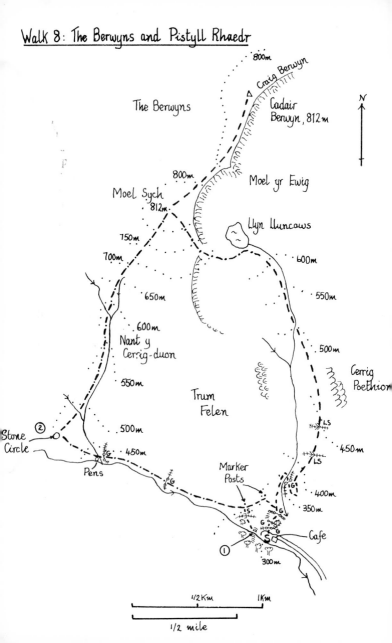

The Berwyns

Craig Berwyn

800m

Cadair Berwyn, 812m

Moel yr Ewig

Moel Sych 812m

Llyn Lluncaws

800m

750m

700m

650m

600m

Nant y Cerrig-duon

550m

Trum Felen

500m

Stone Circle ②

450m

Pens

G

G

Marker Posts

600m

550m

500m

450m

Cerrig Poethion

LS

LS

G

400m

350m

S

G

G

G

Cafe

①

300m

N

1/2 Km   1 Km

1/2 mile

moorland vegetation are some interesting megalithic monuments (see (2) Moorland Berwyn).

From the stones follow an indistinct path downwards to reach a gate above the stream. Beyond the path above the stream becomes gradually more distinct. As the start is approached, the noise of Pistyll Rhaeadr is heard, and an arrowed path, look for the marker post, to the right can be followed to the top of the falls. An exposed viewpoint can be reached, though it is the exposure rather than the view that is exciting, the falls being too steep for a realistic view down it. Return to the main track, and continue along it until a steep, stepped path, again look for the marker post, leads off rightwards. Follow this to join the outward route that is then followed back to the car-park.

(1) *Pistyll Rhaeadr*
Pistyll is Welsh for spout, while *rhaeadr* translates as waterfall, and Spouting Waterfall is an entirely appropriate description for Britain's highest falls south of the Scottish Highlands. The water of the Afon Disgynfa drops 75 m (245 ft) in two fine drops. The first drop is nearly vertical, and at its base the water disappears behind a natural arch, emerging from it as a spout before falling, again almost vertically, into the river – now the Afon Rhaeadr! – below. Geologically the falls are very young, having been born only about 10,000 years ago as a result of ice sculpting in the last Ice Age. A consequence of this youth is the verticality of the falls which have yet to cut back their head and, hence, smooth the drop.

There have been many visitors to Pistyll Rhaedr and each has described the falls. In many ways they are beyond description, a pure sensation of noise and spray, but one of the better attempts was made by George Borrow in his *Wild Wales*, the narrative of a journey around Wales he made in 1854. Borrow is not my favourite writer on Wales; his bullying interrogations of the simple countryfolk he met and his intolerance are not endearing qualities. Occasionally, however, his lyrical descriptions of the scenery are very moving. Of Pistyll Rhaeadr he wrote: 'What shall I liken it to? I scarcely know, unless to an immense skein of silk agitated and disturbed by tempestuous blasts, or to the long tail of a grey courser

at furious speed. Through the profusion of long silvery threads or hairs, or what look such, I could here and there see the black sides of the crag down which the Rhyadr precipitated itself with something between a boom and a roar'.

The valley leading down from Pistyll Rhaeadr to Llanrhaeadr is a fine one, offering hedgerows and trees that shelter an amazing variety of birds. There are tits and warblers, and many other common species, but watch also for nuthatches, tree creepers, pied flycatchers and redstarts. The river itself is also home to the dipper, that most remarkable of water birds, while the cackling call of the green woodpecker is often heard.

(2) *Moorland Berwyn*

The megaliths half hidden among the bracken and moorland scrub are some of the most intriguing in North Wales. 'Megalith' is perhaps a bit of an exaggeration for stones only a couple of feet high, but here is one of the few stone alignments in Wales, and also one of the few stone circles. Familiarity with Stonehenge and Avebury, and knowledge of the existence of other similar, though smaller, sites such as Castlerigg in Cumbria, leads to the opinion that such sites are the norm when, in fact, in many areas they are not.

Here, at Rhos-y-Beddau, is a fascinating series of stones. Look first for the cairn, at 0592 3024. From it go north-east for 40 m to find the start of the alignment. The alignment runs for 60 m to finish at a half-circle of stones. To my knowledge no one, as yet, has pondered the potential astronomical significance of the site: it is an enigma.

On these moors, Celtic legend has it, Arawn, King of the Underworld hunted the souls of the dead with his hounds. His hounds, snow-white except for red ears, could be heard on the high moor, and those who have been held fast in heather that is devoid of tracks, tenacious and, apparently, thigh-deep, while the rain reduces visibility, could be forgiven for believing that the moaning of the wind was the sound of Arawn's pack.

That wind can be cold as well as wet and, in addition, can be

Pistyll Rhaeadr

downright unseasonal. It was known locally as Gwynt Traed y Meirw, the Wind from the Feet of the Dead, a most telling description, and it blew on rich and poor alike. In August 1165 Henry II was campaigning in Wales and crossed the Berwyn moors. August is high summer, but the king faced a driving wind, cold and relentless, blowing equally cold rain. It was more than he could bear. We read that after 'a few days he was oppressed by a mighty tempest of wind and exceeding great torrents of rain' and that he became 'filled with a mighty rage' and 'caused to be blinded hostages who had been held in fetters by him'.

The moorland vegetation that I rather disparagingly referred to as scrub above is, in fact, a fascinating mix of plants, some far from common and worth a few moments of time. The ground cover comprises, chiefly, common heather, but interspersed with it are the low, pink-flowered cowberry, whose red berry is very edible, the crowberry with its tiny pink flowers and berry that turns from green to pink and then gets darker to finish almost black, and the cranberry with its dark shaped flowers, and a fruit so feared by turkeys!

Keep looking and you will find a couple of rarities. One is the cloudberry, which produces a glorious flower, erect and pure white, and which is found only on the high Berwyns, being a plant otherwise restricted to the north – northern Britain that is, not North Wales. That it was a rarity was obviously known to the locals of the Berwyn foothills: one tradition has it that anyone who could give the vicar a quart of cloudberries – the berries are orange when ripe, with many grouped at the head of a flower stalk – was excused all church tithes for a year.

Finally, keep an eye open for the lesser twayblade, a member of the orchid family, barely 5 cm (2 ins) high and with a small, delicate, reddish flower.

The Tanat Valley from the stone circle

Snowdonia

It is thought that the name Snowdon is a very ancient one, perhaps even dating from the Dark Ages, having been given to the upland area of North Wales by seafarers on the Irish Sea who saw the outline of the Snowy Hills as a welcoming landmark. Why these southerly and, frankly, not frequently snow-clad hills should have gained this name in preference to the hills of, say, the Lake District, is by no means clear. Perhaps the more frequented trade route was Ireland-Wales or – and this is supported by evidence from other sources – winters were colder and harsher then, and snow on the hills more common.

Whatever the reason, Llywelyn Fawr – Llywelyn the Great – gave himself the title Dominus Snaudoniae in the first third of the thirteenth century, a title that translates as Lord of Snowdonia even if the spelling is a little ancient. Clearly what Llywelyn had in mind was Gwynedd, of whose royal house he was a prince, the choice of Snowdonia as a lordship probably being in recognition of the significance of the high hills as his best defence. Llywelyn therefore, in common with the sailors, meant all of the mountains of what is now the National Park and, most likely, Lleyn's Yr Eifl as well. Only later did Snowdon contract, firstly to include just the northern groups of peaks – what are now called Snowdon, the Glyders and the Carneddau – and later still, when it was realised that the highest peak was also the highest in mainland Britain south of Hadrian's Wall, to the single peak now popularly known as Snowdon. In Welsh the three upland areas that include the highest peaks are known as Eryri, that name also being used in the Welsh version of the National Park's name. Eryri means, as every book on North Wales tells us, Land of Eagles. So often is this meaning given that it seems sacrilegious to question it, but let us anyway. In Welsh, eagle is *eryr*, so the meaning of Eryri seems obvious. But *eira* is Welsh for snow, and as the name Snowdon is very ancient, could it be that Eryri is a Welsh version of Snowdon, and means Land of Snow? Alternatively, it must be noted that Llywelyn's title is given in Latin, and that the Latin *oriri* means to rise, as in mountains rising. So is the name Eryri derived from the Latin, Land of Mountains?

Finally, and just for light relief, that rarely self-doubting but nonetheless worthy etymologist, George Borrow, claimed the name meant an 'excrescence or scrofulous eruption'! I think that means jagged hills.

The structure of the hill ranges, their wildlife and history, will be discussed in the sections on the individual walks. Here we make some brief, general comments on the area's history, dealing with several excellent historic sites that are not visited on the walks. The pre-history of North Wales has been covered in detail in the chapters on Anglesey and the Lleyn peninsula. While these chapters were specific to their areas, the comments they made were also true more generally. Early settlement of the Snowdonian area was along the coastal strips, where we find the majority of the remaining sites. Chief among these are the burial chambers that lie in the shelter of the Rhinog ridge, near Dyffryn Ardudwy. Three separate sites attract the eye, each one having been called the finest by different scholars at different times. Gors-y-Gedol, and the Dyffryn chambers, are visited on Walk 31, but the Carneddau Hengwm lie off any of our walks. This pair of cairns, at 614 205, must, when complete, have been one of the finest sets of burial chambers in Britain, but sadly they have been dismantled at various times – not for religious reasons, to eliminate traces of paganism, but by use as a convenient quarry, to fashion dry-stone walls. The southernmost monument is 60 m (197 ft) long and 20 m (66 ft) wide, huge by any standards, and though the northern cairn is smaller, it is still a massive monument.

Elsewhere in Snowdonia, two other chambers do not conform to the theory that all early settlers lived on the coastal strip. At Capel Garmon (818 543) there is a fine three-chambered tomb, now in the care of Cadw, which has been thoroughly investigated, but remains well preserved. More evocative is Maen-y-Bardd, the Stone of the Bard, that stands high on the flank of Bwlch y Ddeufaen, the pass over the north-eastern arm of the Carneddau. This monument, at 740 718, is a small, but very well preserved, cromlech. Near it and apparently aligned with it are a pair of standing stones which are newer – probably Bronze Age – and which gave the pass its name. The effect of these stones on the walker who has crossed the Bwlch

– a beautiful pass, once crossed by the Romans, but not enhanced by the transmission lines, which prevent it from being a Best Walk – is profound, and raises all sorts of questions. The answer to the obvious one of why here, on this high, cold, weatherswept hill, is that probably the cromlech was raised in a forest not on a bare hill.

Of the Bronze Age there are two remarkable reminders, in addition to several smaller sites. One of these reminders is a Bronze Age road, taken on Walk 28, that passes many monuments from the time, including one that was, until vandalised, probably the finest of the area's Bronze Age sites. The other excellent reminder is another road, which goes south of the Cregennen Lakes before skirting Cadair Idris on its northern side.

Of Iron Age remains, nothing in Snowdonia compares with the site of Tre'r Ceiri (see Walk 4), though several hilltop sites do exist. Pen-y-Gaer is a fort, unlike Tre'r Ceiri whose status is ambiguous. The site, at 750 693, is heavily fortified with three rings of rampart and ditch defences; the outermost is not complete, but the inside ring is still 4.5 m (15 ft) thick. Most interesting of all are the two areas of *chevaux de frise*, pointed stones set into the ground to make life painful for a would-be attacker who would have been poorly shod. A few hut circles have been found at Pen-y-gaer – these can be seen from the Maen-y-Bardd burial chamber – but neither here nor at the Conwy Mountain site (see Walk 19), which also has the foundations for hut circles, is there anything comparable to Tre'r Ceiri.

Elsewhere there are small sites, chiefly of interest to the specialist, such as the Celtic field systems in Cwm Pennant and Cwmystradllyn. If the Celtic remains are less imposing than those elsewhere, the same is not true of the Roman remains. The finest site is at Caernarfon, outside the boundary of the National Park, at 482 624, near the A487 Caernarfon-Beddgelert road which crosses the site. The site has been extensively excavated, and the remains of barracks, bath-houses etc. are open to the public. There is also a museum. Although it is believed that the site had a wooden fort at first, the stone buildings we now see were erected around the time of Agricola's expedition of AD 78. It was then occupied, though probably not continuously, for about 300 years.

From Segontium, a road ran over Bwlch-y-Ddeufaen to the fort
of Canovium, at 776 703, while another road ran southward to
Tomen-y-mur, a fort that must have competed with that below
Lakeland's Hard Knott Pass as the remotest in Britain. This fort,
also completed during Agricola's campaign, stands at 707 388,
though the site is now dominated by a Norman motte, suggesting
that the road it marked was important for 1000 years. To the
north-east of the fort site there is a small circular earthwork
sometimes described as an amphitheatre, but more likely, from its
size, to have been a cock-pit. The road past Tomen-y-mur is Sarn
Helen, one of several with that name, said to derive from *sarn*,
causeway, and Elin, the daughter of the British king Gratian, who
married the Roman emperor Magnus Maximus at the end of the
fourth century AD and persuaded him to build roads across Wales.
In reality the roads pre-date the emperor, Gratian is a legendary
king, and the name is probably a corruption of *sarn y lleng*,
causeway of the legion. Facts can be very cruel.

From the time of the departure of the Romans to the coming of
the Normans, the history of the Celts in Wales is one of hard-won
unity and fragmentation, a succession of inter-tribal, eventually
inter-kingdom, wars for short-lived supremacy. This civil-warring is
the more strange considering the name the Welsh have given their
country. Following the battles of Dyrham and Chester (see the
introduction to the Anglesey chapter) the isolated Celts drew the
security blanket of comradeship around them, calling themselves
Cymry, fellow countrymen, and their land Cymru. To the Saxons at
the border of their land, they were Wallas, foreigners. The name
probably derives from Velcae, a Celtic tribe known to the Germanic
Saxons, and is the root not only of Wales, but of Walloon in
Belgium, of Valais in Switzerland and of Vlachs in Romania.

Faced with such a threat the Celts would, you might think, close
ranks literally, rather than just linguistically, but not so. One
problem was undoubtedly the system of *gavelkind*, the division of a
man's land between his sons upon his death. This system does not
work well when the land in question is a few acres of mountainside,
sibling rivalry being what it is, but when the land is a kingdom it is
doomed. For centuries the history of Wales is one of attempts to

unify the country by the currently strongest leader, the obliteration of his efforts after his death, and the violence of the civil wars becoming ingrained, so that when a united front was required, none was possible.

In all of this Gwynedd, the northern kingdom conforming very roughly to the present county's boundary, was invariably the strongest fragment. One king of Gwynedd was Maelgwn, called 'the Island [Anglesey, that is] Dragon . . . first in evil, mightier than many in power and malice' by Gildas, the sixth-century writer. Maelgwn died in AD 547 to the clear delight of Gildas – a monk, called The Wise by his contemporaries, and many different things since – who even found a moral in his passing. This man, this evil, God-provoking tyrant, 'beheld the Yellow Plague through the key-hole of the church door and forthwith died'. But evil though Maelgwn, may have been, and it is after all a relative term when applied to politics, especially power politics, the great strength of the Gwynedd he left sustained its ruling princes for three centuries. Eventually he was surpassed in unifying attempts by Rhodri Mawr, Rhodri the Great, the last of a line. Rhodri united Wales from Anglesey to Plynlimon, defended his land against the Viking raiders – a victory of his in a battle on Anglesey was praised in the Carolingian court of Charles the Bold – but found that the great mountain defences of his kingdom also sealed it off from South Wales and hindered unity. Rhodri was killed in a skirmish with the Saxons and, as his death coincided with the rise to power of Alfred the Great, his successor, Anarawd, felt the need to submit to this new, powerful king, journeying to his Wessex court to do so.

The next Welsh prince to attempt to unify the Welsh was Hywel Dda, Hywel the Good, a prince of Ceredegion (Cardigan) who, by marriage and violence, conquered Gwynedd and Powys, but failed to secure the south. Hywel is remembered for having codified Welsh law. He also defined many things that had been too long matters of debate, even if his definitions were occasionally eccentric. Gold plate, he decreed, had to be 'as thick as the nail of a ploughman who has been a ploughman for seven years'.

Finally Grufydd ap Llywelyn ap Siesyllt – ap means son of – unified the country in 1041, the only Welsh king to do so, although

it can be claimed that the unified country was less independent than
the smaller 'country' of Llywelyn the Great. Grufydd almost
immediately committed the foolishness of assuming that the Saxons
were like the Celts, and could be fragmented. Sensing greatness he
attempted to form alliances with Saxon border earls. Earl Harold
Godwinson – soon to be victor at Stamford Bridge and loser at
Hastings – was told, and given permission by Edward the
Confessor, to mount a punitive raid. Grufydd retreated to his
Gwynedd stronghold, but Harold was no mean general. He selected
a force of battle-hardened troops and took on mountains, weather
and Grufydd, defeating all three. Wales fragmented in the wake of
Grufydd's death and when next a man sought unity he found a
different race at the border, the Normans.

The Normans were of sterner stuff than the Saxons, who had
been content to stay behind Offa's Dyke as long as the Welsh
behaved. The Normans installed their Marcher Lords and took
anything they felt was worth having, specifically South and
mid-Wales and much of what is now Clwyd. They did not want
Gwynedd or most of Powys, so the Welsh could have those – if they
were quiet. Owain Gwynedd was not quiet and succeeded, for a
time, in pushing the Normans out of Powys, assisted, as we have
seen on Walk 8, by some typical Welsh weather on the Berwyns.

Owain's grandson, Llywelyn ap Iorwerth, re-established
Gwynedd – fragmented, as usual, by the king's death – and by being
in the right place at the right time succeeded in gaining rights for the
Welsh. The English king at this time was John and Llywelyn
married his illegitimate daughter, Joan, following which he sided
with the barons against his father-in-law, gaining concessions in
Magna Carta. Though Llywelyn – known by the Welsh as Llywelyn
Fawr, Llywelyn the Great – did not succeed in unifying Wales, he
did succeed in bringing true independence to the large part he
controlled.

Llywelyn the Great never called himself Prince of Wales,
referring to himself only as Prince of Aberffraw and Lord of
Snowdon, but his son, Dafydd, did assume the title Prince of Wales.
Dafydd fought a long and very hard civil war to defend Gwynedd,
Llywelyn the Great's unity unravelling behind him, and war

followed Dafydd's death, the prince having been childless.
Grandsons of Llywelyn the Great, sons born to Grufydd,
Llywelyn's eldest son by a Welsh woman, fought, and of these
grandsons, Llywelyn ap Grufydd, Llywelyn the Last, achieved
supremacy. Llywelyn, seizing the opportunity offered by the
rebellion of Simon de Montfort, regained land from the Marcher
Lords, and succeeded in forcing the English king Henry III to sign
the Treaty of Montgomery in 1267, giving Llywelyn the title Prince
of Wales, and defining a principality favourable to the Welsh.
Sadly, Henry III was succeeded by Edward I, a far more formidable
foe, who invaded Wales and forced Llywelyn to pay homage and to
sign the Treaty of Aberconwy in 1277, which reduced him to the
position of a baron. When, five years later, Llywelyn rose in
rebellion there was no great war, the prince being killed, alone in a
small, forgettable skirmish near Brecon, by an English soldier who
did not even realise whom he had speared. Dafydd, Llywelyn's
brother, held out a little longer, but was captured, tried for treason
and executed.

Following the deaths of Llywelyn and Dafydd, Wales was kept
quiet for a century until the rebellion of Owain Glyndŵr dealt with
in the chapter on his homeland, the Berwyn and Clwydian Hills.
After another century Henry VII emerged from a Gwynedd
background to take the crown of England and lay the ground for the
Acts of Union of Henry VIII, greatest of the Tudor kings. Henry
VII, Henry Tudor, was the grandson of Catherine of France, wife of
Henry V, who had married Owen Tudor, a Gwynedd 'commoner',
after the death of her husband the king. Henry Tudor's father
Edmund – son of Catherine and Owen Tudor – married Margaret
Beaufort whose family line stretched back to Henry IV, But good
though his bloodstock was, it is doubtful if Henry Tudor would have
succeeded in his claim to the Lancastrian crown if many of the
Yorkist supporters had not found themselves greatly alarmed and
appalled by the new king Richard III. The House of York had won
the Wars of the Roses, but when their king, Richard, was on the
field of Bosworth he lacked not only a horse, but an army.

In Gwynedd the last princes had built several castles, but these
cannot compare with the Edwardian 'Ring of Stone' castles. There

is Dolbadarn, a single round tower near Llanberis, and
Dolwyddelan, a single square tower in the Lledr valley. One,
however, has a feel to it that is different. Castell-y-Bere, which we
shall visit on Walk 35, is a ruin: there is no grand sweep of stone to
inspire the visitor, no detail of drawbridge or portcullis,
embattlement or murder hole to thrill him. But there is a distant
view of high Cadair Idris, part of the natural defence of Gwynedd,
and a closer view of green countryside. Here in this quiet valley, a
castle signifying the independence of the Welsh spirit stands amidst
land defining Wales.

THE SNOWDONIA NATIONAL PARK

The National Parks and Access to the Countryside Act of 1949
empowered a newly formed National Parks Commission to set up
Parks in England and Wales. In 1951 the Commission designated
the Snowdonia National Park, second largest of the ten that were to
be created, and one of three in Wales.

The Park is, roughly, diamond shaped, bordered by the Dyfi
valley to the south, the line of the Conwy valley to the east, and the
coasts to the north and west, except that from near Bangor the
border cuts inland to take the northern and western edges of the hill
ranges, thus excluding the Lleyn peninsula. Also excluded is a
central 'hole' in the Park, around Blaenau Ffestiniog. The Park
covers 2150 sq km (838 sq miles) and has a permanent population of
around 25 000. The land is largely privately owned (about 70 per
cent), mostly upland sheep-farming land, the remainder being held
chiefly by the Forestry Commission (about 16 per cent) and the
National Trust (about 9 per cent). The Forestry Commission has
planted about 75 per cent of its holding – that is about 12 per cent of
the Park area – this lying chiefly in three large forests, the Gwydyr
to the west of Betws-y-Coed, the Coed-y-Brenin, astride the A470
Dolgellau-Ffestiniog road, and the Dyfi along the river north of
Machynlleth. These forests hold valley positions, the tree-line in
North Wales being about 550 m (1800 ft).

As we shall see, in part at least, on our walks, the Park holds

some amazingly diverse scenery, from the rock peak of Tryfan through the grassy whalebacks of the Carneddau to the 'soft' river valley scenery of the Dyfi and the sand dunes of Morfa Harlech, and shows a range of monuments to man's interest in the area from neolithic burial chambers to Trawsfynydd's nuclear power station.

In addition to the nuclear power station, there are several other power stations within the Park. Cwm Dyli is hydro-powered, the huge tubes that take water to the station being clearly visible along Walk 10. The Dinorwig, near Llanberis, and Ffestiniog stations are pumped-storage. Electricity, particularly the high-voltage, high-power alternating current form generated in modern power stations and exported via the National Grid's overhead transmission lines, is not amenable to storage in its 'as manufactured' state. This is not a particular problem when the generating plant is flexible – at night you close a few plants down. Nuclear stations and the larger conventional stations are much less flexible and have to be kept running, presenting a problem with night-time over-capacity. The pumped-storage plant is one answer, night-time generation being used to lift water from a lower to a higher reservoir, the day-time need for extra power being satisfied by allowing the water to flow back downhill generating electricity by the usual hydro-power route. The Ffestiniog plant uses Llyn Tanygrisiau as the lower lake, Llyn Stwlan as the upper. Dinorwig uses Llyn Peris and the Marchlyn Mawr reservoir. At the latter site there is no dam-wall dominating the view in the way that the Stwlan dam does, but each of the top lakes can show the 'tide-mark' to which all reservoirs are prone.

Elsewhere, Park industry is limited to 'country crafts' and other light varieties. The railways are unobtrusive, except for the one to Snowdon's summit, and offer excellent rides. The British Rail lines, from Deganwy to Blaenau Ffestiniog and the Cambrian Coast line, offer splendid views, and the 'little train' services are equally good, the trip from Porthmadog to Blaenau Ffestiniog passing through some inspiring lowland scenery.

The Park's natural history is varied, though the cool, damp

Y Lliwedd from Llynau Mymbyr

climate discourages many birds and animals. Those that do live in the Park have the advantage of a relatively undisturbed habitat. Pine martens and fallow deer still live in the Coed-y-Brenin Forest, and on more open ground there are badger, fox and hare. The Park's birdlife includes, on the hills, ring ouzels and, for the very lucky, choughs. Elsewhere it is a somewhat limited list, if the sight of a buzzard working the thermals above a ridge, or the harsh call of a raven can ever be called limited. Craig yr Aderyn (Bird Rock), south of Cadair Idris, does offer a remarkable sight – cormorants nesting on an inland crag. It is likely that the sea once came this far and Craig yr Aderyn was a sea cliff. The more dedicated ornithologist should not miss the RSPB's Ynys-hir site, just outside the Park border, south of Machynlleth.

Most remarkably the common frog can be found at heights that seem astonishing. I once found one as I neared Llyn Clyd, below Y Garn's final pyramid, at a height of about 600 m (1950 ft). That, I thought, was surely as high as they go, but there are proven finds 1000 ft higher on Carnedd Llywelyn!

In 1639 a London pharmacist called Thomas Johnson climbed Snowdon to see what plants he might discover, and he did this not as a herbalist, although he was one, but for the joy of botanical discovery. Snowdon is, therefore, the first British mountain to have been botanically explored. Before the end of the century Johnson had been followed by several other enthusiasts. In 1798 two keen amateurs, The Reverends Bingley and Williams, approached the formidable Clogwyn du'r Arddu intent on unlocking the secrets of its flora. Complete with picnic basket they scrambled up the earthy terrace that splits the cliff diagonally, ascending from right to left. Half-way up they realised that they could not get down, but 'there seemed no chance of our being able to proceed much further, on account of the increasing size of the masses of rock above us'. Luckily though, Revd Williams 'having a pair of strong shoes with nails in them, which would hold their footing better than mine, requested to make the first attempt, and after some difficulty he succeeded'. Revd Bingley followed by pulling on the first man's belt! They continued and after 'about an hour and a quarter from the commencement of our labour, we found ourselves on the brow of this dreadful precipice'. Bingley added, with obvious satisfaction, that the men were 'in possession of all the plants we expected to find'! At one stroke the two clerics had advanced the cause of Snowdonian botany, and invented the sport of rock climbing. It must be said, however, that climbing for its own sake was many more years in coming and that the Eastern Terrace has no real place in the history of the sport, although the feat still draws admiring comments from those who know of it.

The flora for which all these men were searching is restricted, in the mountain areas of the Park, to the steeper cliffs, away from the predations of wind and sheep. There, the purple saxifrage is an early bloomer, followed by two other saxifrages with white flowers. The Snowdon Lily, the Park's most famous plant, that grows nowhere else in Britain, is restricted to the cliffs of Snowdon and the Glyders, and is rarely seen except by rock climbers and the very ardent botanist, though I have known visitors who claim to have seen it with binoculars from more accessible parts of the hills. Snowdonia also holds the Killarney, alpine woodsia and holly ferns, each very rare and, sadly, becoming rarer because of over-collecting. Elsewhere, in sheltered spots it is possible to find Welsh poppy, violets, primroses and ox-eye daisies.

In the lower regions of the Park the growth is more substantial and more varied. There are bogs holding sundews and asphodel, beautiful oakwoods with ancient flower carpets, and interesting lake and river shores. There is also the very pleasant but increasingly threatening rhododendron, which has escaped from gardens and is both thriving and spreading. Excellent though the plant is, and good though the cover it affords bird and animal life, it would be sad if its spread were to endanger natural Welsh habitats.

The Park has sixteen National Nature Reserves within its borders, some of which require permits before they can be visited. These can be obtained from the Nature Conservancy Council in Bangor (see Useful Addresses). The reserves, five mountain, nine woodland and two coastal sites, are:

Snowdon. No permit required. See Walk 11.
Cwm Idwal. No permit required. See Walk 14.

Cwm Glas, Crafnant. Permit required for fenced woodland. See
Walk 12.

Rhinog. No permit required. See Walk 29.

Cadair Idris. Permit required for fenced woodland. See Walk 34.

Coedydd Aber. No permit required. See Walk 18.

Coed Gorswen (755 708). Permit required to leave public footpath
through wood. Wood comprises wych elm, ash, hazel and
pedunculate oak with excellent 'damp-floor' flora.

Coed Dolgarrog (768 665). Permit required. Pedunculate oak,
sessile oak, beech, elm, sycamore and alder wood. Variety of
floor-covering flora from dry to wet, including several orchids.

Coed Tremadog (562 402). Permit required. Reserve includes cliffs
on which climbing is not permitted, and the mixed deciduous woods
above them. Good collection of ground cover, cliff plants and ferns.

Coed Camlyn (657 398). Permit required. Mixed deciduous woods
with damp cliffs. Ground cover includes bilberry, but occasionally
spoiled by bramble.

Coed Cymerau (688 428). Permit required. Fine oakwood site
including gorge with ferns and mosses.

Coedydd Maentwrog (650 403). No permit required. Pair of sites
near Plas Tan-y-bwlch, the National Park Study Centre, and the
Tan-y-bwlch station of the Festiniog Railway. Mixed deciduous
woodland with dry floor covering.

Coed y Rhygen (680 370). Permit required. A reminder of the
ancient oakwoods of Gwynedd. Particularly fine collection of ferns.

Coed Ganllwyd. No permit required. See Walk 32.

Morfa Harlech, north of Harlech. Permit required for part of the
reserve. Astonishing mix of habitats, from seaweeds to marram
grass to orchid-rich, fertile soil. Many species of insects, and birds.

Morfa Dyffryn, north-west of Dyffryn Ardudwy. Permit required
away from public footpaths. Another site with habitats from
seaweed to orchids. Again, many insects.

SNOWDON

The geology of the Snowdonia National Park is extremely complex. Here we consider only the salient features of each of the hill groups that make up the Park, so that the overall physical geography of the area can be understood.

As we have seen in the Anglesey chapter, the oldest Welsh rocks are pre-Cambrian, that is older than 600 million years. At that time the Park area was the floor of an ocean, and on to that ocean's floor the rocks of the Cambrian, Ordovician and Silurian eras were deposited. Deposition took about 200 million years, a huge thickness being laid down on a floor that sagged under its weight and, therefore, remained under water. In passing it is worth noting that all the names so far are Welsh in origin – Cambria, a romantic name given to the area, Ordovician from the Celtic tribe of the Ordovices who held Gwynedd, and Silurian from the Celtic Silures who held the country south of Gwynedd.

During the time the Ordovician rocks were being deposited there was considerable volcanic activity in what was to become the Park. The volcanoes formed a curved line across the Park, starting at Cadair Idris, then moving through the Arans, the Arenigs and the Moelwyns to Moel Hebog. From there the line straightened, going through Snowdon, the Glyders and along the Carneddau from Carnedd Llywelyn to Foel Fras. Some of these volcanoes almost certainly appeared above the sea as the traditional cones, but in general the activity was more subdued, fissures emitting lava in constant flows rather than in spectacular outpourings. Interestingly the volcanoes did not produce granite as they frequently did elsewhere, but a material called tuff, built of a compressed mixture of dust and ashes. It is of this rock (tough by nature as well as name!) that the rock peaks of the Park are formed.

At the end of the Silurian era a series of earth movements called the Caledonian Orogeny thrust the ocean floor upwards, exposing the rocks. In addition to its general upward thrust, the movement squeezed the rock beds. The principal squeeze, from a point of view of the Park's structure, was with the masses of Snowdon and Cadair Idris, each with its hard volcanic rock, as terminal points. As they moved closer, the rock beds between them were pushed upward into what is known as an anticline. A further effect of the pressure was to align all of the internal particles of the rock which had previously been randomly scattered. When ordered in this way the rock is easily cleaved to form slates, and at each end of the anticline there were, indeed, slate quarries, at Llanberis, Bethesda and Abergynolwyn.

Once exposed, the rocks started to weather, the softer Ordovician and Silurian strata being removed to leave the volcanic tuff. The Ice Ages assisted this process, on Snowdon creating a magnificent series of hollows that the Welsh call *cwms*. Five such cwms exist, separated by ridges that are never broad, frequently knife-edged. It is those ridges and cwms that are followed on our walks.

Walk 9   The Snowdon Horseshoe

This walk takes the two most obvious knife-edge ridges, those two enclosing the finest of the cwms. It is a magnificent route, certainly the best in Wales, and ranking with the best in Britain. The ascent of Crib Goch, and the traverse of its Pinnacles, are steep and exposed, no place for the nervous or the absolute beginner. In winter conditions the route is a very serious undertaking and should only be attempted by those who are both experienced and well-equipped.

Walk category: Difficult (4½ hours).

Length: 12 km (7½ miles).

Ascent: 1000 m (3300 ft).

Maps: Landranger Sheet 115; Outdoor Leisure Sheet 17.

Starting and finishing point: The car-park at Pen-y-Pass (647 557) at the top of the Llanberis Pass.

From the car-park (see (1) Pen-y-Pass) the obvious exit is the Miners' Track (Walk 10) Our walk leaves by an exit in the car-park's right wall, taking a path that goes behind the café, and heads towards the Llanberis Pass. This is the Pig Track (see (2) Pig Track), and it is followed straightforwardly as it climbs diagonally across the mountain to reach the obvious pass of Bwlch Moch. Ahead now are two paths, the left one being a continuation of the Pig Track that avoids the high ridge *en route* to Snowdon's summit. Our path is the slab-marked right-hand one that rises deceptively slowly at first, but then rears up to present a real challenge. There is a path of sorts marked out by the passage of boots so that it has become clean and slightly lighter than the surrounding grey rock, but the walker can also pick his own way. The last few feet to the summit of Crib Goch are steep and exposed, the summit itself, when reached, being equally exposed, but offering outstanding views into the Llanberis Pass, Cwm Glas and into the great hollow that the Horseshoe defines.

Ahead, the ridge is knife-edged, and best negotiated on its left side away from the near-vertical drop into Cwm Uchaf. The Pinnacles stand astride the ridge and are not easily turned, but with care they can be safely crossed to reach Bwlch Coch, which separates Crib Goch from Crib-y-ddisgl. The walk to the triangulation pillar on the summit of Crib-y-ddisgl is more leisurely, with only the occasional rock step. The summit is a broad one, the view from it now dominated by the cliffs of Clogwyn y Garnedd that form the eastern face of Yr Wyddfa, as the highest peak is more correctly called.

The descent from Crib-y-ddisgl to Bwlch Glas is straightforward, and from there the path follows the railway to the summit of Yr Wyddfa (see (3) Snowdon Mountain railway). Some find it easier to walk on the railway sleepers, others – like the author, whose inside leg measurement is so short that his stride length is exactly wrong – take the path (see (4) Yr Wyddfa). From the summit of Yr Wyddfa go south – that is, head off along the summit café building with the railway at your back. The route is down, over a steep slope of loose rock, the path, such as it occasionally is, needing some care. The path ends on Bwlch y Saethau (see (5) Bwlch y Saethau). The pass

Walks 9-12 Snowdon

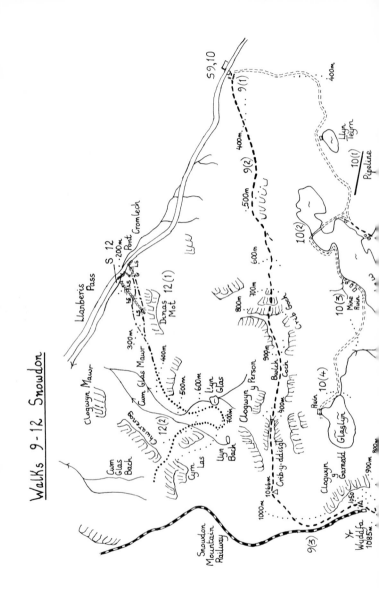

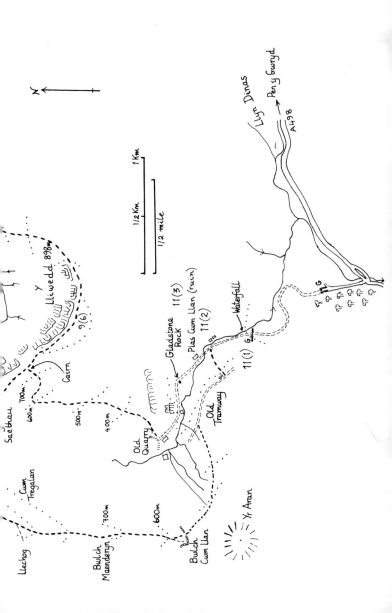

is wide and long, and near its far end an obvious path goes upward towards Y Lliwedd, leaving an equally obvious one (the Watkin Path, see Walk 11) ascending from the south-west.

The traverse of Y Lliwedd with its twin rock-tower summits is straightforward, although it should be borne in mind that the cliff face that falls from the summit most of the way to Llyn Llydaw is the highest in Wales. Others may be steeper, but none is longer (see (6) Y Lliwedd). Beyond the summits a conspicuous path leads gently down towards Llyn Llydaw and the Miners' Track that is followed back to the Pen-y-Pass car-park.

(1) *Pen-y-Pass*

Before a road was laid over the Llanberis Pass in the early years of the nineteenth century, Pen-y-Pass had to be reached on foot. It must have been an impressive place then, with the wide valley stretched out below uncontaminated by tarmac. It certainly impressed one visitor: 'A perpetual unbroken sabbath stillness reigns through the vast profound, except that at intervals, the piercing cry of the kite or the minstrelsy of the stream is heard.' This comment seems almost religious in its early words, and this reverence is something that I have met elsewhere in people as they talk of the hills. In complete contrast someone else noted that area was 'irregular and rough and full of quagmires'!

The first hotel, fitted neatly into a sheltered cleft in the rock, followed shortly after completion of the road. In the early years of this century a larger hotel, the Gorphwysfa, replaced the earliest, its tenant Owen Rawson Owen staying until his death in 1962. He is remembered, as is his most famous early guest, Geoffrey Winthrop Young, on slate tablets near the door of what is now a youth hostel. The café across from the old hotel is a very recent addition.

(2) *Pig Track*

Much ink has been used in the discussion of the derivation of the name Pig. Some say Pig because it reaches Bwlch Moch, the Pass of the Pig, but *moch* could be from quick not pig, denoting a quick way into Cwm Dyli. Pig does not, in fact, need an explanation, say

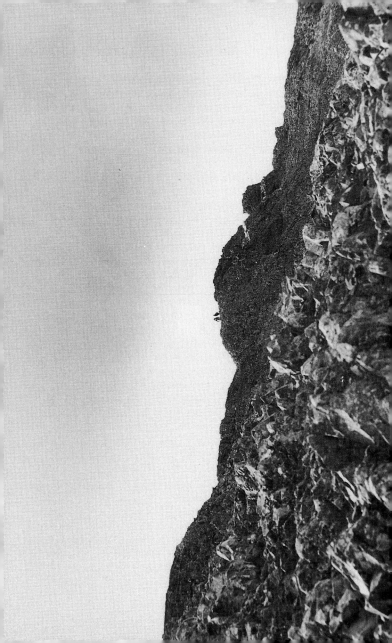

others: since *pig* is Welsh for peak, it is the Path to the Peak – but
where does that leave us with *moch*? Pig and *moch* seem too similar
to be unattached. Yet others say Pyg not Pig, from Pen-y-Gwryd,
the hotel beyond Pen-y-Pass, but Pig pre-dates the hotel, so that is
unlikely to be true.

Crib Goch is easier. That means the Red Comb, comb as in
cock's comb, or Red Ridge.

(3) *Snowdon Mountain Railway*

The rail link from Llanberis to the summit of Yr Wyddfa was
completed in the remarkable time of thirteen months in the 1890s.
The official opening on Easter Monday 1896 was marred by the only
serious accident in the railway's history and one that led, sadly, to
the only death to have occurred. The two trains that had travelled to
the summit that day were returning when the engine of the first left
the line, uncoupled itself and crashed down the mountainside,
narrowly missing some walkers who must have wondered what it
was they had eaten to cause the sort of nightmare that involves
being run down by a train while walking up a mountainside. The
coaches were halted, but not before one passenger had jumped
clear, breaking both his legs. The second train ran into the coaches,
but no one else was hurt. The injured man was taken to hospital,
but died there.

The track is 8 km (5 miles) long; the gauge 2 ft 7½ ins, which is
not amenable to metrication. The average gradient is about 1 in 7,
the steepest 1 in 5½. A speed limit of 5 m.p.h. applies, so on a
good, clear day the scenery can be thoroughly enjoyed.

There can be no doubt that the train's existence does allow some
who would not visit the summit, the elderly and infirm, to reach it
but I always have mixed feelings about the whole venture,
especially the café at the top. I was once made to feel out of place
there, in my wet weather gear and boots, among all the ill-clad
tourists. It was an odd sensation.

(4) *Yr Wyddfa*

The highest peak's name translates as The Grave, though this name
is, correctly, applied only to the final pyramid. On this peak lived a
giant, Rhito Gawr, whose hobby was cutting beards from
passers-by, the beards being used as a cloak to ward off winter's

chills. One day Rhito tried to cut off Arthur's beard, but the incensed hero cut off the giant's head. His body fell here where, in time, earth and rock covered it.

(5) *Bwlch y Saethau*

The Pass of the Arrows, as the Welsh name translates, is also linked with Arthur. Here Arthur fought his final battle when, accompanied by the last of his remaining Knights of the Round Table, he faced Mordred, some renegade knights and an army of Saxons hired by Mordred. Some versions of the story have the evil Mordred as Arthur's nephew, in others he is his son: it is good versus evil, the old against the young. In the battle Arthur cuts a path through his enemies to reach Mordred who strikes him first, fatally wounding him. With the last of his strength Arthur wields Excalibur above his head, bringing it down on Mordred, splitting his head apart. As is required by such stories, Mordred dies screaming, while Arthur waits quietly for his own death (see note (4) of Walk 10).

(6) *Y Lliwedd*

The north-facing cliffs of Y Lliwedd, steep, though not sheer, and long – about 300 m (1000 ft) – attracted a great deal of attention in the early days of Welsh rock climbing. Here Archer Thompson, Geoffrey Winthrop Young and George Leigh Mallory (later to disappear near the summit of Everest) climbed, and a guidebook to the cliff was the first such guide published. Today the hard climbs are elsewhere, but Lliwedd still gets the occasional visit from those for whom tradition is not a dirty word.

Walk 10   The Miners' Track

This route is an accepted way to Snowdon's summit, but we shall not go that far, contenting ourselves with reaching Glaslyn, a dark lake below the cliffs of Clogwyn y Garnedd, Yr Wyddfa's huge north-eastern face. Those with children will find this walk to be an excellent introduction to mountain scenery and to the 'feel' of big hills, with plenty to do and see.

Walk category: Easy/Intermediate (2½ hours).

Length: 10 km (6¼ miles).

Ascent: 300 m (1000 ft).

Maps: Landranger Sheet 115; Outdoor Leisure Sheet 17.

Starting and finishing point: As for Walk 9 above.

In terms of direction-finding no route in this book is easier, a broad, sometimes flagged, path extending from the car-park at Pen-y-Pass all the way to the end point of Glaslyn.

From the car-park the path rises gently, curving equally gently to lose the view back to Pen-y-Pass. Beyond little Llyn Teyrn, the pipes taking water to the hydroelectric power station can be seen (see (1) Cwm Dyli Power Station). Beyond the pipelines the view opens up into Cwm Dyli, and the path descends briefly to a causeway constructed across the eastern end of Llyn Llydaw (see (2) Llyn Llydaw Causeway). Beyond, the ruins of the old mining buildings are reached (see (3) Brittania Copper Mine). There are more ruins at Glaslyn, which is reached beyond a steep section of path. In the latter stages of the walk to Glaslyn, the Afon Glaslyn draining the top lake into Llyn Llydaw shares the same ground as the path. As a result, after prolonged or heavy rain the path can be interesting.

From Glaslyn (see (4) Glaslyn) the zigzag path to Bwlch Glas, and so to Yr Wyddfa, is obvious, but we reverse our outward route back to the car-park.

(1) *Cwm Dyli Power Station*
The hydroelectric power station is situated at 653 540 and is connected by about 2.5 km (1½ miles) of double piping to Llyn Llydaw. The pipes are 2½ ft in diameter, were laid in 1906, and feed three turbines that generate 5 megawatts (that is 5 000 000 watts) of

Yr Wyddfa from the Miners' Track

power. This power output is tiny by modern standards, but the fuel is free and usually available in excess. Snowdonia has one of the highest rainfalls in Britain, and the only other ingredient of the power station's fuel is gravity which has not, as yet, been known to fail.

The buildings beside Llyn Teyrn, near where we first see the pipeline, are the ruins of the miners' barracks, the men who worked Cwm Dyli's copper being housed here during the week and travelling home to their families only at weekends.

(2) *Llyn Llydaw Causeway*

The story of the causeway is told on an inscribed slate slab beside it:

> The Llydaw Causeway was built by the Cwmdyle Rock and Green Lake Copper Mining Company under the direction of the mine captain, Thomas Colliver. During its construction the level of the lake was lowered 12 feet and 6,000 cubic yards of waste rock from the mine was used to build the embankment. The causeway was first crossed on 13 October 1853.

Despite the lowering of the lake level the causeway was occasionally flooded, and in recent times, to prevent this, it has been raised to the original lake water level.

(3) *Brittania Copper Mine*

The Llyn Llydaw Causeway was built to aid the removal of copper ore from the Cwm Dyli mines to Pen-y-Pass. If you are tired when you reach the main buildings, spare a thought for the men who carried the ore in sacks on their backs, sparing even more of a thought when you realise that before the opening of the causeway the ore was back-packed to Bwlch Glas, and sledged down from there to Rhyd-ddu. The men's work was usually cold and wet, always dangerous, and their barracks at night were far from home. An account of the mining notes that on one winter's day in 1801 the men dug through drifting snow to reach the mine: in one place the snow was 60 ft deep.

Copper was worked in Britain from earliest times – bronze is an alloy of copper and tin – and certainly worked in Cwm Dyli from the.

Mining ruins and Llyn Llydaw

late eighteenth century through to 1926. The mine itself is beside
the zigzag path on the hillside above Glaslyn. Beside the lake are
more barracks. Beside Llyn Llydaw is the ore-crushing building, an
eerie place of groaning winds.
(4) *Glaslyn*
Glaslyn, a mysterious dark lake nestling close to sheer cliffs, is the
home of one legend, and my favoured spot for another.

Glaslyn – the Blue Lake, a modern corruption of the old name
Llyn Ffynnon Las, the Lake of the Blue Spring – is home to the
afanc, a Welsh water monster. The tale is that the monster, all
scales and sharp bits, lived in the Conwy river where it made a
nuisance of itself by flooding the area, periodically drowning
livestock and making people homeless, and readily disposing of
anyone sent to kill it. The *afanc* was also partial to young girls one
of whom, brave beyond measure, lured it from the river and cradled
its hideous head in her lap. Thus relaxed it was overcome by nets
and chains. Oxen were then used to drag it to Glaslyn, where it
remains to this day.

The story seems to be based on the beaver – known as *efync*, or
water monster in some old tales – whose damming habits might
easily have led to a flash flood of the Conwy valley if a dam failed.
Of course it is said that recently an angler fishing Glaslyn hooked
something very large that gave him a quick glimpse of teeth so huge
that . . .

Following the battle at the Bwlch y Saethau Sir Bedevere carried
the fatally wounded Arthur to the shores of Llyn Llydaw and laid
him down. Ordered by the king to throw Excalibur into a named
lake, Bedevere left him. But which lake? Most stories have Idwal or
Ogwen, but they are too far. I prefer Glaslyn, close at hand and
with as much mystery as is required. Bedevere twice hid Excalibur
and was called a liar when he returned to Arthur saying he had seen
nothing. On the third occasion he threw the sword and an arm rose
from the lake, the hand clasping the sword, waving it three times
and disappearing. When told, Arthur lay silent and a black boat
carrying three young women emerged from the mist on Llydaw to
take him to Avalon where his fatal wound could be healed.
Bedevere led the remaining knights to a cave in Lliwedd's cliff.

Years later a shepherd wandering under the cliffs of Lliwedd looking for lost sheep found a cave and, when he entered it, was astonished to see a king asleep on a rock slab, a great jewelled sword beside him and knights asleep around him. Retreating, afraid, the man knocked his head on a bell and at its ring the king awoke and asked, 'Is it time?' 'No, sleep on,' said the shepherd, and the king nodded. 'I will sleep on,' he said, 'until it is time to rise and free my people in Britain.' The shepherd went out, and was never able to find the cave again.

Walk 11   The Watkin Path

This route starts through some fine downland scenery which makes the extra climbing very worthwhile. However the top section of the walk – reversing the descent of Walk 9 – is steep and loose, and needs great care. Those attempting the walk in winter should be both experienced and well equipped.

Walk category: Difficult (5 hours).

Length: 14½ km (9 miles).

Ascent: 1100 m (3600 ft).

Maps: Landranger Sheet 115; Outdoor Leisure Sheet 17.

Starting and finishing point: The lay-by car-park at Pont Bethania (628 506) on the A498 Capel Curig-Beddgelert road, between the twin lakes of Dinas and Gwynant.

Use the old Bethania bridge in the lay-by to cross the Afon Glaslyn, and then cross the main road to take a lane – signed footpath to Snowdon and reached over a cattle grid – northward. The lane goes to a farm, but we leave it on a rougher track to the left which is an old mine and quarry road. This path soon opens up superb views to the waterfalls and fine scenery in the lower part of Cwm Llan.
    When the waterfall is reached a gate in the wall allows access to

the Cwm y Llan Nature Reserve (see (1) Cwm y Llan Nature Reserve). Across the river here are the ruins of a copper ore processing building, the ore having been produced in mines on the hillside separating Cwm y Llan from Cwm Meirch.

Beyond are the ruins of Plas Cwm Llan (see (2) South Snowdon Slate Works). The path eases now, and at the end of this flatter section the large *roche moutonnée* to the left is Gladstone Rock (see (3) Watkin Path and Gladstone Rock). Beyond the Rock there is an excellent slab of rock to the right, opposite which is a ruin from the slate-working days. Around the corner are more ruins, and huge tips associated with the slate quarrying.

Above the slate tips the path becomes increasingly steep and difficult until Bwlch Ciliau is reached and the path to/from Y Lliwedd is joined. Beyond is Bwlch y Saethau (see note (5) of Walk 9), above which is a steep and very difficult path to the summit of Yr Wyddfa (see note (4) of Walk 9).

On descending, reverse the path towards Bwlch y Saethau for about 150 m to a conspicuous pointed rock, where another path goes off south-west (rightwards as you descend). Take this path, which descends the less tricky Bwlch Main. After walking about 700 m, and having descended about 150 m (500 ft), you will reach another path junction. Bear left, descending easy-angled ground. Care is needed here, particularly if visibility is poor, as the path is less well defined than some to Snowdon's summit, and the cliffs of Clogwyn Du to our left (east) would be nasty to fall over. In good visibility the views out over them into Cwm Tregalan and across to Bwlch y Saethau and Y Lliwedd are excellent. That to the west is equally good, with the Nantlle ridge in semi-profile and Mynydd Mawr above Llyn Cwellyn. Ahead, Yr Aran is a fine peak, and those with the time should consider climbing it, as it offers an unrivalled view of the whole length of the Watkin Path. Near the bottom of our descent, towards Bwlch Cwm y Llan which separates this long ridge of Yr Wyddfa from Yr Aran, an indistinct path, left, descends a scree slope and uses a gap in a wall to gain open ground. Cross this on an indistinct path to join the broad terrace of land that once

carried the slate works' tramway. Go right (south) along the tramway, and after a surprising bridge, take the path left (north-east) that descends steeply to join the Watkin Path just south of the ruins of Plas Cwm Llan. From here, the path is followed back to the car-park.

(1) *Cwm y Llan Nature Reserve*
The reserve covers 1680 hectares (4150 acres) and was established for its geological interest, and for its plant life. On Craig Ddu, the fine slab outcrop beyond Gladstone Rock mentioned in the walk directions, there is a fine collection of heathers, scarce elsewhere because of extensive sheep grazing. Near the slate tips there are also fine clusters of parsley fern.

(2) *South Snowdon Slate Works*
The quarry opened in 1840, but work lasted only 40 years. The chief difficulty was the cost of transportation from the site to the docks of Porthmadog. From the quarry horse-drawn trams took the slates to the top of an incline (passed three times on the early part of the route), where they were lowered to Pont Bethania. From there they were carted to Porthmadog. There were plans for a railway or tramway, but the slate was not of the highest quality and the quarry closed. Plas Cwm Llan is the ruin of the mine manager's house, the bullet holes in its walls dating from D-Day training in 1944. The house is in a very dangerous state and should not be entered.

    The ruins nearer the slate tips are of the workers' barracks.

(3) *Watkin Path and Gladstone Rock*
The Watkin Path was given to the nation in 1892 by Sir Edward Watkin, the railway magnate – chiefly remembered for his attempt to dig a Channel tunnel, an attempt aborted by the government of the day – who lived near Pont Bethania. To open the path Sir Edward persuaded Gladstone, then 83 and Prime Minister for the fourth time, down from London. Gladstone and his wife travelled by open car from Caernarfon in pouring rain, and walked to this spot in weather no less atrocious for the opening ceremony. The Prime Minister addressed a large crowd on the subject of 'The Land Question in Wales', a choir sang and, at Gladstone's request, sang an encore. Then everyone went home to dry out. During the whole

proceedings not one word was said about the Watkin Path! To make amends a small group walked the path again the following day, though only Gladstone's wife, with a guide, reached the summit.

Gladstone Rock, which has an inscribed plaque detailing the events of 13 September 1892, is a magnificent example of a *roche moutonnée*, a 'rock sheep', as such glacially attacked boulders are known. The uphill side is beautifully smoothed by the glacial ice, while the downhill side has had large chunks of rock plucked out by scouring ice.

Walk 12   Cwm Glas

Of the five great cwms bitten from the peaks of Snowdon, Cwm Glas is the least frequented, but the most 'mountainous'. The ground is rugged, and the paths few, and for that reason the route, though short, is not classified as Easy.

Walk category: Easy/Intermediate (2½ hours).

Length: 6 km (3¾ miles).

Ascent: 450 m (1650 ft).

Maps: Landranger Sheet 115; Outdoor Leisure Sheet 17.

Starting and finishing point: The lay-by car-park at 628 567 in the Llanberis Pass just below the Pont Cromlech, the bridge over the Afon Nant Peris.

Go up the pass, crossing the Pont Cromlech, to reach a gate and ladder stile to the right. Beyond, a sometimes poorly defined path reaches a ladder stile, or climbs steeply to the cliff of Dinas Mot (see (1) Dinas Mot). Go over the ladder stile, skirt around the base of the cliff and climb over increasingly difficult ground into Cwm Glas itself (see (2) Cwm Glas). Return by the same route.

(1) *Dinas Mot*

This cliff forms the blunted end of Crib Goch's north ridge, a massive blockhouse of a cliff not surprisingly named as a fortress (*dinas*, fortress) and equally unsurprisingly attributed to a giant, Mot. The most noticeable feature of the cliff is the huge, detached, monolithic nose – called by climbers 'The Nose' with a directness not always apparent in their naming – below which the path to Cwm Glas winds.

(2) *Cwm Glas*

Cwm Glas, in fact two cwms divided by the ridge of Chwarenog, the larger one of the south, is a paradise for plant lovers, the abundance and variety of species that grow here being astonishing. The cwm is hemmed in by huge and impressive cliffs. The black and damp Craig y Rhaeadr guards the entrance, while the massive 200 m (650 ft) Cyrn Las forms its back. To the left as we walk up the cwm the retaining wall is that of the first ridge of the Horseshoe route (Walk 9), with the Pinnacles of Crib Goch well defined. One word of advice here is to note the position of Clogwyn y Person, the 80 m (250 ft) cliff which stands out northward from the ridge just to the east of the summit of Crib-y-ddisgl. More than one walker, tricked by mist and false trails, has walked off the Parsons' Cliff to oblivion rather than on towards Bwlch Coch.

Cwm Glas holds two small lakes, Llyn Glas and Llyn Bach, each finely situated and adding contrast to the rocks.

In short, in any direction, from any point of view Cwm Glas is magnificent.

THE GLYDERS

The name Glyder almost certainly derives from *cludr*, meaning a rock pile, a name entirely appropriate to the summit areas of both Glyder Fawr and Glyder Fach, and for the Castle of the Winds between them. Geologically the Glyders are little different from Snowdon at the southern (true eastern) end, except for the amount

The Llanberis Pass

of slab rock lying about on the summits. Tryfan, a superb comb of a mountain and probably Wales's most famous peak after Yr Wyddfa itself, is certainly as fine and as rocky a peak as Crib Goch or Y Lliwedd. At the northern end of the range, however, more rolling scenery predominates. But there, the effects of the Ice Age are dramatic and have created a different, but no less superb, landscape. Nant Ffrancon, as the valley of the Afon Ogwen below the obvious rock step at the Ogwen Cottage is called, is a classical example of a glaciated, U-shaped, valley. As the glacier scoured the valley, other smaller ice-fields formed in the hollows of the northern Glyders that formed the western ridge of the valley. These cwms, widened and deepened it is believed by a rotational movement of the ice, became more pronounced because they face north-east, and therefore accumulated more snow, and were truncated by the main valley glacier. After the glacier had disappeared only the more southerly cwms, most notably Cwm Idwal, were overdeepened and moraine-blocked sufficiently to allow lake formation, but the geography of the western face of the northern Glyders is extraordinary enough without lakes. The cwms, six in total counting Cwm Idwal as the first, then one facing north beyond Carnedd y Filiast, and Marchlyn Mawr below Elidir Fawr, have formed narrow ridges between them producing a series of steep finger ridges which join in delicate, almost overhanging tops. Foel Goch is the best example, but Mynydd Perfedd and Carnedd y Filiast are each delightful.

Walk 13   Tryfan and Bristly Ridge

Not quite in the Snowdon Horseshoe class, but nevertheless a fine walk, taking in the best of the Glyders' scrambling ridges.

Tryfan

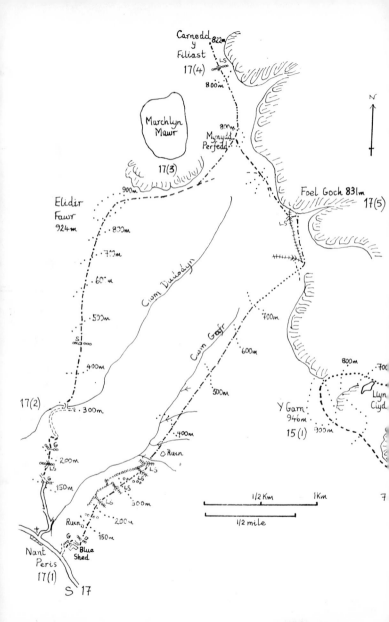

Walk 13-17 The Glyders

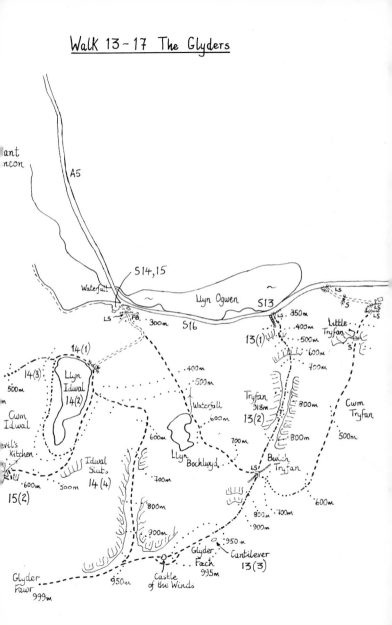

Walk category: Difficult (3¾ hours).

Length: 9.5 km (6 miles).

Ascent: 950 m (3100 ft).

Maps: Landranger Sheet 115; Outdoor Leisure Sheet 17.

Starting and finishing point: Any of the numerous lay-bys on the A5 beside Llyn Ogwen.

On the blunt end of Tryfan's north ridge a clean, tall buttress of rock (Milestone Buttress) stands out about 50 m (160 ft) above the road. From the left-hand end of this buttress a stone wall takes a steep, direct line to the road fence. At its base is a ladder stile. Go over this, and follow the wall upward. This wall is a masterpiece of the wall-builder's art. In places it is awkward to stand, let alone to build strong walls. As the wall finishes (see (1) Milestone Buttress) go left and upwards to gain the north ridge proper. The north ridge is now followed to the summit by a path that is sometimes indistinct and occasionally devious. The way is never difficult, unless made so, but is always interesting. It is not knife-edged, as Crib Goch is, but a little meandering captures the best of the views, and they are good, into Cwm Bochlwyd and Cwm Tryfan, to the right (west) and left (east) respectively. At one point the Cannon – a leaning slab of rock – is reached, a feature that is so obvious from the Ogwen Cottage.

The summit (see (2) Tryfan) is dominated by two blocks of stone which are frequently mistaken for people when viewed by tourists on the A5. From it go down by any reasonable route to Bwlch Tryfan which is crossed by another fine stone wall. A ladder stile helps the walker here. Ahead is Bristly Ridge which, if the standard of the walk is to be maintained, should be taken head-on. To its left, an alternative scramble takes a swept path up steepish scree. We follow the wall to its end and go 10 m to the right to a gully. Beyond it is another gully that rears up towards its top. Avoid the steep

The Cannon, Tryfan

section by exiting left on to its ridge. Beyond, easier ground leads to a flat top, a good place to view the Great Pinnacle. Cross the gap to it, climbing to its right to a further gap, beyond which is easy ground.

Before Glyder Fach's shambles of a summit, be sure to visit the (much-visited) cantilever about 250 m from the top, and to the left of the path (see (3) Glyder Fach). From Glyder Fach take the obvious path to Castell y Gwynt (the Castle of the Winds) which is traversed with less difficulty and interest than looks likely at first, although the drop from its right side demands respect. Continue to the top of Glyder Fawr.

Reverse the route to the top of Y Gribin, a prominent shoulder to the north of the low point on the Fach-Fawr ridge. Descend the ridge, with care at first, but then over easier ground. From the base of the ridge it is straightforward to break right to Llyn Bochlwyd, following the path from it to the Ogwen Cottage, but it always feels more satisfactory to take a path leftward to the Cwm Idwal path (see Walk 14). This does add 1200 m of roadwork, but has the advantage of passing the tea-shop.

(1) *Milestone Buttress*

The buttress was named from a real milestone that once stood on the road below it, the spot being 10 miles from Bangor. Once one of the famous cliffs of British climbing – so famous that it became almost a household name and was featured in a book, *Murder on the Milestone Buttress* – it is now thought to be a very moderate place, for beginners and others.

(2) *Tryfan*

The two 2 m (6 ft) blocks of rock on the summit were not raised as cairns by climbers, but are a natural formation, Tryfan's lava having formed into columnar ribs from which softer rock has weathered. The stones are called Adam and Eve, and traditionally Adam is the larger although there is no anatomical detail to support this. Also traditionally, anyone who steps from one block to the other receives the Freedom of Tryfan. Be careful if tempted; the drop to the east is not trivial.

Glyder Fawr and the Castle of the Winds from Glyder Fach

(3) *Glyder Fach*

The cantilever is about 7 m (23 ft) long with about 2.5 m (8 ft)
overhanging its last pivot point. Thomas Pennant visited it in 1778,
drawing it for his book, and the drawing suggests that it has not
changed position at all in 200 years. There are rumours that
schoolchildren by the dozen have sat on its end and it can only be
hoped that no party ever manages, by trial or error, to tip it.

Charles Kingsley, after he had visited Glyder Fach, wrote of 'that
enormous desolation, the dead bones of the oldest born in time'.
That seems a bit black to me – Glyder Fach is a real fairground of a
summit.

Castell y Gwynt, the Castle of the Winds, is poetically named,
and is a charming jumble. In the right wind conditions the stones do
hum gently, like great organ pipes, and as sunset approaches and
the shadows lengthen the light patterns are equally symphonic.

Walk 14   Cwm Idwal

The gentlest walk on the Glyders, but a very fine and rewarding
one, maintaining its interest and with excellent views.

Walk category: Easy (1 hour).

Length: 4.5 km (2¾ miles).

Ascent: 90 m (300 ft).

Maps: Landranger Sheet 115; Outdoor Leisure Sheet 17.

Starting and finishing point: Lay-bys and car-parks at the Ogwen
Cottage (650 603) or the tea-shop beside it.

Go up the minor road from the main A5 – or, if starting from the
tea-shop car-park, go towards the A5 – and take the signed,
constructed path going south-east. A very fine and narrow cleft in
the rock to the right shortly is worthy of a moment of your time.

Ahead, the path takes one of a pair of stiles over a fence, then crosses a nicely sited footbridge, and continues straightforwardly to a gate in a fence. Beyond is Cwm Idwal and its nature reserve (see (1) Cwm Idwal).

Go through the gate and go right on a path that hugs the lake (see (2) Llyn Idwal) at first, then leaves it to go among hummocks of glacial debris (see (3) Moraine). As the far end of the lake is reached, the path heads off towards the Devil's Kitchen ahead (see note (2) on Walk 15). Here go across the peaty land at the lake's tip, taking great care to avoid damage by keeping to the rocky margin, to reach the Idwal Slabs (see (4) Idwal Slabs). Here take a path that leads easily back to the entrance gate to the reserve, and reverse the outward route.

(1) *Cwm Idwal*

The cwm is owned by the National Trust but has been leased as a National Nature Reserve by the Nature Conservancy Council since 1954. When inside the reserve please do not damage or uproot any plants, and do not enter the fenced enclosures. The reserve is grazed by sheep and occasionally by feral (that is once domestic, now wild) goats, although these tend to stay among the upper crags in summer. Because of the heavy grazing, the plant varieties are limited, but interesting: the more inaccessible nooks and crannies hold purple saxifrage and mountain sorrel, a number of semi-rare ferns, including green spleenwort, and some interesting lichens. In the boggy areas of the lake grow sundew and butterwort, two insectivorous plants.

(2) *Llyn Idwal*

Llyn Idwal is very shallow over most of its area, rarely more than 3 m (10 ft) and never more than 10 m (35 ft) deep. Its bottom is a thick layer of peat and mud as much as 4 m (13 ft) thick. Trout and minnows live in the lake which, in winter, occasionally provides a resting site for ducks and swans.

The lake is named after the son of Owain Gwynedd, reputedly drowned here by his foster parents. Legend has it that because of this no bird will fly over the lake, a legend which, while disproved by the resting ducks, does reflect reality in that there are few birds in the reserve.

(3) *Moraine*
The long hummocks between the lake and the cwm edge are glacial
moraine, debris brought down by the Cwm Idwal and Y Garn
glaciers, and left behind when the ice retreated. Among the
hummocks are some textbook quality *roches moutonnées*, rocks
whose up-glacier (uphill) side is smoothed, but whose downhill side
is steep and indented, plucked away by the glacial dragging.
(4) *Idwal Slabs*
The Slabs have been a beginner's playground for generations of
climbers, the low angle making the routes (comparatively) easy
while the shortage of holds teaches balance. A retaining wall – to
the left if the slabs are viewed head-on – has routes that are far from
easy, one of which, Suicide Wall, Route 1, was the first Welsh
'extreme': the first ascent was by Preston, Morsley and Haines on
7 October 1945.

Walk 15   Y Garn and the Devil's Kitchen

This walk includes the fine hanging cwm beneath Y Garn's final
pyramid, and one of Wales's best clefts. Though short for a
'difficult' category climb, the descent of the Devil's Kitchen requires
care and good route-finding. *This descent is not recommended in
winter conditions.*

Walk category: Difficult (3 hours).

Length: 8 km (5 miles).

Ascent: 700 m (2300 ft).

Maps: Landranger Sheet 115; Outdoor Leisure Sheet 17.

Starting and finishing point: As for Walk 14.

The stream beside the path to Cwm Idwal

Follow Walk 14 around the northern end of Llyn Idwal, from where a path can be picked up by going right (north) to the edge of the cwm. This path takes the right (north) ridge of Y Garn, offering a safe but, in places, steep way to the summit. It is better to follow the stream that flows into the northern end of Llyn Idwal from the hanging cwm under Y Garn, Cwm Clyd. This trackless ascent is less steep than the ridge path, and covers some interesting ground. It does, however, pass through the nature reserve, and great care must be taken not to destroy vegetation.

From Cwm Clyd, with its very pleasantly sited lake, nestling in its glacial hollow, the ascent of Y Garn is steep by any route. To the right (north) the ridge path can be regained, or a rock ridge defined gully can be used to gain the summit ridge. To the left the ground is steep, though broken, and can be ascended, with care. (See (1) Y Garn.)

From the summit of Y Garn descend the southern ridge to Llyn y Cŵn, the Lake of the Hounds, a remote, windswept piece of water set among part boggy, part stony ground. This was the scene of a famous mountain ghost story (see (2) Devil's Kitchen). When the mist comes down, and the Devil's Kitchen cleft opens wide in readiness to nibble away at the unwary, this is a desolate spot. Was that the wind, or the noise of the Hounds?

The Devil's Kitchen cannot be descended, and care must be taken to locate the right descent path. From the lake go north-east to find a shallow, stony gully that leads to the correct path. This path is quite wide at first, but it narrows as it traverses diagonally across the retaining cliff of the Kitchen. To reach the base of the cleft, it is necessary to do a small amount of scrambling. From the base of the cleft go down to join paths going to each side of Llyn Idwal. Take the right-hand path to the Idwal Slabs, and then return as for Walk 14.

(1) Y Garn

Because of its position the summit of Y Garn commands a superb view, across Cwm Idwal to Tryfan and the Glyders, over the

Y Garn from Cwm Idwal

northern Glyders to Nant Francon, out across the Llanberis Pass to
Snowdon, and across the Ogwen valley to the high peaks of the
Carneddau.

(2) *Devil's Kitchen*

In Welsh this is Twll Du, the Black Hole, a large cleft, deep enough
to be dark, glistening and dripping with water from Llyn y Cŵn.
From the top, a flat platform near where the stream falls offers an
excellent view, but do not attempt to climb down the cleft. There is
a famous story of a lone walker who met another, also solitary,
walker near Llyn y Cŵn and after talking offered to walk down the
footpath with him. The man leapt away, saying 'No, no. I must go
down,' and disappeared into the mist towards the Devil's Kitchen,
refusing to heed shouted warnings. The story-teller descended the
path and, finding no sign of the other, walked back alone to Ogwen.
When he inquired if they had seen the other man there he was told
that, the day before, the man he had described had been killed
when, after taking the wrong path, he had fallen down Twll Du.

The Devil's Kitchen was first climbed in winter as long ago as
1895 with the help of a hatchet as ice axe! It was three more years
before it received a summer ascent. The route is graded 'V. Diff.'
but it is a dank, confined V. Diff. and not to be toyed with. The
descent path we used is known as Llwybr Carw, Deer Path,
suggesting that Cwm Idwal was once home to more than sheep and
goats.

Walk 16   Cwm Bochlwyd and Cwm Tryfan

This route is a circumnavigation of Tryfan, a worthwhile objective
in its own right, but also taking in two magnificent cwms, tight
Bochlwyd and open Tryfan.

Walk category: Intermediate (2¾ hours).

Length: 8 km (5 miles).

Ascent: 450 m (1500 ft).

Maps: Landranger Sheet 115; Outdoor Leisure Sheet 17.

Starting and finishing point: Any lay-by or car-park on the A5 beside Llyn Ogwen.

From your start point reach the Ogwen Cottage and follow Walk 14 until the obvious right-angled bed in the Cwm Idwal path, about 200 m beyond the footbridge. There a distinct but unmade path leads off in a direction that is a continuation of path from the footbridge, heading for Bwlch Tryfan.

Soon, the Bochlwyd falls can be seen ahead, not spectacular but pleasant enough: the path goes to their right and can be very wet. Beyond the falls, Cwm Bochlwyd opens up, with the marvellously enclosed glacially-formed lake of the same name filling its floor. The skyline across the lake takes in a sweep of the high Glyder ridge, the Castle of the Winds standing out especially well.

Cross the outflow stream to go round to the left of the lake on a path that ascends easily to Bwlch Tryfan. Those who have not yet completed Walk 13 get a fine view of the Bristly Ridge from here, to whet the appetite. Take the ladder stile over the wall at the pass and take the path that curves around the head of Cwm Tryfan. After about 400 m, with, all the while, Tryfan's east face opening up and view down the broad and long Cwm Tryfan improving, a path going down the cwm will be seen. The two paths do not quite merge on a scree slope, so choose a convenient point to join the cwm path. The cwm is a delight, not only for the view of Tryfan's fine east face, crossed diagonally by the Heather Terrace, an outing well worth considering at some stage, but for the more local views, a jumble of rock, water, moss and heather. At the fence use the stile to join a path to the farm, Gwern Gof Uchaf. There go left along a broad track that was the valley road until the construction of the A5 in the early nineteenth century. Above left from here is Tryfan Bach, Little Tryfan, usually alive with aspirant rock climbers.

Walk 17   Cwm Dudodyn and the Northern Glyders

Cwm Dudodyn is a long, sheltered and extremely pretty valley reaching upwards towards the pass between Elidir Fawr and Foel Goch, and offers an excellent way of reaching these two peaks and of exploring the sculpted geography of the other northern Glyder peaks. The walker can also see into Marchlyn Mawr, to assess for himself the effect on the environment of the new CEGB power station.

Walk category: Difficult (5¼ hours).

Length: 15 km (9½ miles).

Ascent: 1150 m (3800 ft).

Maps: Landranger Sheet 115; Outdoor Leisure Sheet 17.

Starting and finishing point: The car-park at 609 580 reached by taking the main Llanberis Pass road. If you are coming down the pass, the car-park is to the left just before the village of Nant Peris.

Cross the car-park to the main road. Go left, through Nant Peris (see (1) Nant Peris) to the chapel on the right. Take the lane to the (right) side of the chapel and follow it around a left-hand bend, and on to a gate. There is a footpath sign here. Go through the gate and continue to a barn on the right, where a gate, right, leads to a path. Follow this, crossing a ladder stile, to a gate and signpost. Go through the gate to a track that is followed around a left-hand bend to the Afon Dudodyn (see (2) Dinorwig quarries). The Afon Dudodyn's valley is a charming place, rowan trees above sparkling water and moss banks.

Cross the Bridge and take one of several indistinct paths beyond that cross a wall and reach Elidir Fawr's summit for a view over the Marchlyn Mawr reservoir (see (3) Dinorwig Power Station).

The Afon Dudodyn

Go north-east to Bwlch y Brecon and climb Mynydd Perfedd (by literal translation of the Welsh, the Hill of the Bowel!) and continue to Carnedd y Filiast (see (4) First viewpoint). Reverse the route over Mynydd Perfedd and climb Foel Goch (see (5) Second viewpoint).

From Foel Goch descend to Bwlch y Cywion and take an indistinct path that leads down Cwm Gafr towards the Llanberis Pass. Beyond a ruin, fences are crossed, and as Nant Peris comes into view a blue shed gives the line. Head for it, going steeply downhill. A hundred feet or so above it, go left past a ruin to a house and wall gap. Go through and down to the shed. Go round right of it to a track that is followed to the main road. Go left for the car park.

(1) *Nant Peris*
Nant Peris is an odd village, a place on the way to other places. Originally it was the Llanberis village, but that moved down the pass when the Dinorwig quarries opened, leaving 'Old Llanberis', as it is sometimes known, behind. The small, medieval church is dedicated to St Peris, but its external charm is not continued inside, where Victorian 'restorers' left little intact.

(2) *Dinorwig quarries*
The first slate quarry to use the terrace method was the Penrhyn in Bethesda, though Thomas Assheton Smith was employing it here in 1809, about 25 years later. The rock was split using gunpowder, which produced a 'soft' explosion and so did not damage the stone. After blasting it was taken to the dressing mills where, after being sawn into usable blocks, it was hand split, a very great skill. An expert could get six slates from an inch of rock. The split slates were then cut to size, various roofing sizes being made. Those interested in the quarrying, which had a fascinating technical, but appalling social, side should not miss the North Wales Quarrying Museum in Llanberis, an excellent site. One noteworthy point is that the terraces had individual, and sometimes exotic, names and that these have been carried forward to the present day, the rock-climbing guide to the area still using them. I wonder if the climbers on the routes in Australia or California are aware of why their slate faces have such odd names.

(3) *Dinorwig Power Station*

The numbers associated with the Dinorwig pumped-storage scheme are staggering. The station is entirely underground in a cavern made by the excavation of 3 million tons of slate. The cavern would accommodate two football pitches, and is as high as a sixteen-storey building. The tunnels to Marchlyn Mawr are 3 km (2 miles) long, and 10 m (33 ft) across. The station uses nearly 1500 million gallons of water in a complete cycle, and can be generating 1320 megawatts – enough for 1 320 000 single bar electric fires – within 10 seconds of switch-on. Marchlyn Mawr's 600 m rockfill dam required nearly 2 million cubic m of infill, to raise the water level by 35 m (105 ft). During a complete cycle the lake water falls to its original level.

So much for the technical. On the aesthetic side, the power station has virtually no impact on the environment, except to create giant tide-marks on the upper and lower lakes, Marchlyn Mawr and Llyn Peris, and this effect is not attractive visually, although it hardly compares with a cooling tower or a fuming chimney. Ethically, as to whether any such development should be allowed within the boundaries of a National Park, I leave the reader to advise himself.

The area of high ridge near Marchlyn Mawr is the home of the Water Horse. It appears friendly when first seen, apparently offering a gentle ride, but once a rider is on its back, it gallops away, hurling itself into the lake. The rider is never seen again.

(4) *First viewpoint*

Carnedd y Filiast, the last significant peak of the Glyders, offers a commanding view over the glaciated Nant Ffrancon, and on over the Menai Straits to Anglesey. Equally good is the view across the northern end of the Carneddau.

(5) *Second viewpoint*

Foel Goch's position, slightly east of the main Glyder ridge, means that it has a virtually uninterrupted view down Nant Ffrancon, and also of the ice-formed cwms on the ridge itself. Yr Esgair, the long, steep and loose ridge descending into Nant Ffrancon from the summit, is, I am told, excellent practice for the Hörnli ridge on the Matterhorn!

THE CARNEDDAU

It would be very tempting to suggest that the Carneddau are the end point of the change from the jagged peak to whaleback ridge as we have moved eastward from Snowdon. It would be tempting because the Glyders did seem to be half-and-half, rocky peak and grassy hump. But it would be wrong. The cliffs of Craig yr Isfa and Ysgolion Duon are as angular and precipitous as anything on Lliwedd or Tryfan; the climb up Pen-yr-ole-wen as wicked as anything on either of the western ranges; the jumble of stones on Bera Bach as good, if not as large, as anything on the Glyders.

It is in their eastern part that the Carneddau really turn to grassy whalebacks, with the high wide ridges of Foel Fras and Drum, Bwlch y Ddeufaen, and the gentler slopes into the sea at Conwy. There are also the curving humps of Pen Llithrig y Wrach and Pen yr Helgi Du, as seen from the A5. In addition, the hills have had a bad press: Thomas Pennant in his *Tour in Wales*, published in 1778, found them 'very disagreeable', all 'dreary bottoms or moory hills', and later visitors have been equally uncomplimentary.

But the Carneddau have much to offer the walker, not least solitude on the eastern side where, despite the very long penetration of valleys formed by streams anxious to get to the Afon Conwy, there are still good spots for the hard worker. In addition, the Carneddau offer a great variety of scenery, in this assisted by the very large area they cover (they form by far the largest of the three great ranges). In the walks below, we explore that scenery.

The Northern Glyders from Glyder Fawr

Walk 18: Aber Falls

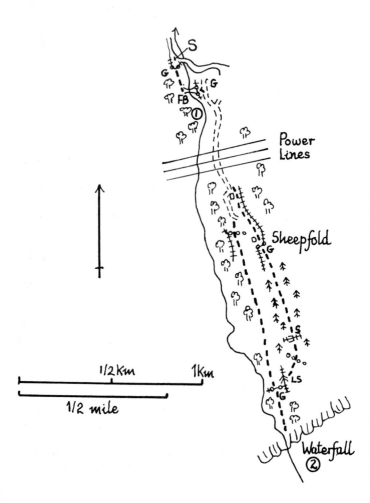

S

G
G
FB
①

Power
Lines

Sheepfold
G

LS

LS
G

Waterfall
②

1/2 Km   1Km

1/2 mile

Walk 18   Aber Falls

This easy walk takes in some superb river scenery, and the falls are the most spectacular in the National Park. Definitely not to be missed.

Walk category: Easy (1¼ hours).

Length: 5 km (3 miles).

Ascent: 150 m (500 ft).

Maps: Landranger Sheet 115; Outdoor Leisure Sheet 17.

Starting and finishing point: Car-park at 662 720, reached from Aber village by a signed road that leaves the village road almost immediately after the village road is entered from the A5. There is a garage at the corner of the main and village roads, a useful landmark. There is a second car-park beyond Bont Newydd if this first, small one is full.

The car-park is beside Bont Newydd, a pretty bridge, which is not crossed. Instead go through a gate, signed for the falls, to reach a riverside path through beautiful woodland that is part of the nature reserve (see (1) Coedydd Aber National Nature Reserve). Indeed, the walk follows, to the falls, part of the Coedydd Aber Trail through the reserve.

The path leads to a footbridge beyond which is a gate. Go through this and take the distinct track beyond. (To the left here a gate gives access to the second car-park, those starting here being advised to go on to the footbridge, for its excellent view of the river.)

Follow the track, going straight ahead at a junction where one track goes off left to a farm. The track bends around a cottage, and then goes off left. Here leave it to go straight on, through a wall gap, to follow the always distinct path to a gate. Beyond it are the falls (see (2) Aber Falls). To return, reverse the outward route or,

for the same mileage, go through the nature reserve woodland to
the east of the outward path. For that route, go back through the
gate and then over the ladder stile to the right to follow a trail on a
distinct path marked with blue-topped stakes. A stile leads to the
wood. At an obvious junction where the blue stakes go right – the
trail leads back to the car-park, adding about 1.25 km (¾ mile) to
the walk length – keep left.

Leave the wood over a stile and go through a wall gap to a path
beside a fence, which leads to the farm track of the outward
journey, just beyond the cottage.

(1) *Coedydd Aber National Nature Reserve*

The reserve is an excellent piece of very well managed mixed
deciduous and conifer wood. There are oak, ash, hazel, alder,
willow and birch near the river and, beyond the footbridge, some
fragrant balsam poplar. Further on, the conifers, chiefly Japanese
larch and Norwegian spruce, have been interplanted with sycamore,
beech and poplar. The success of this is seen in spring when the
forest floor is alive with colour, chiefly from primrose, bluebell and
wood sorrel.

On the return journey the more organised conifer plantation can
be seen. On the medium slopes there is sitka spruce, while on the
highest land – the highest land that will support conifer, that is – the
spruce is replaced by lodgepole pine. The success of the whole
reserve is indicated by the (relative) abundance of birds, with some
fine uncommon species being represented, nuthatch and tree
creeper on the bark, siskin and goldcrest among the branches.

(2) *Aber Falls*

These falls, in Welsh Rhaeadr Fawr, the Big Waterfall, are 35 m
(115 ft), and were produced when the river, attempting to cut back
its head, hit a band of hard rock. In this case the hard rock is
granophyre, which is an uncommon rock among Snowdonia's
igneous outcrops. The cliffs to the sides of the falls, being
unreachable by sheep, support an excellent array of damp-loving
plants, chiefly mosses and liverworts.

Aber Falls

To the left (east) of the falls there is a fine scree slope about 90 m (300 ft) high, the scree having been formed by frost erosion of the rock mass of the two Bera peaks – Bera Mawr and Bera Bach, the Large and Small Haystacks – that form the backdrop to distant views of the falls.

Walk 19   Conwy Mountain and the Sychnant Pass

This fine walk is at the extreme tip of the Carneddau range, where the mountains fall into the sea. Conwy is a delightful place, its medieval town walls and castle being the best examples of their kind in Wales, and the Sychnant Pass is one of the 'Great Passes of Wales', often pictured on holiday postcards.

Walk category: Intermediate (2¾ hours).

Length: 10 km (6¼ miles).

Ascent: 350 m (1150 ft).

Maps: Landranger Sheet 115; Outdoor Sheet 16.

Starting and finishing point: Conwy Castle, using any of the village car-parks.

From the castle take Rose Hill Street, pass the square, and then take Upper Gate Street (signposted for the Sychnant Pass) to the left to pass through Porth Uchaf, the south-western gate in the town's medieval walls (see (1) Conwy). After about 100 m, bear right on the road signed 'Sychnant'.

After passing the last road (of new houses and bungalows) to the left go about 200 m, passing weight-limit and end-of-speed-limit signs, to a signed footpath left. Take this (indistinct) path to a kissing gate in the fence (right). Continue obviously to a lane. Here

Conwy, Castle and Bridge

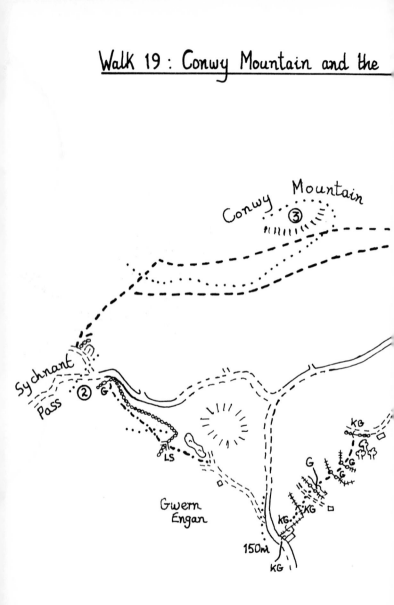

Conwy Mountain

③

Sychnant Pass

② G

LS

Gwern
Engan

KG

G

KG

KG

KG

G

KG

G

150M

KG

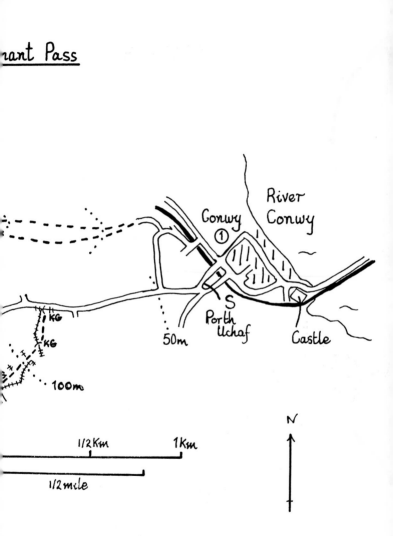

rant Pass

River
Conwy

Conwy
①

KG

KG

50m

S
Porth
Uchaf

Castle

100m

N

1/2 Km   1 Km

1/2 mile

go right and almost immediately left, near a post-box, on a lane between some fine houses. Follow the lane until it curves rightward when woodland is reached. Here go left along the wood edge, and continue along a more indistinct path. At a new track to a new house go over the track and up and left to a kissing gate. Now follow the field edge, left, past boggy ground to a lane, exiting via an odd corridor between a fence and a house. Go right. After a short distance take the signed path left, at the 'No cars or motorcycles' sign, for Pen y Bwlch. After a short rise leave the track, which goes to Gwern Engan farm, to take a path to the left of a lake. Go over a wall and follow the wood edge, right to the top of the Sychnant Pass (see (2) Sychnant Pass).

Go left on the metalled road for a very short distance to a track, right, going uphill. This becomes metalled, and passes below some good rock outcrops to an elbow of walls. Right here, along the wall, leads more directly to Conwy, but we go on, taking the top of the ridge through the hill-fort (see (3) Castell Caer Leion). Beyond, the path remains distinct leading to the Machno Cottages. Go down the lane past the cottages, turning right at a sign to Conwy Mountain. Go along the road, turning left at the T-junction, and take the bridge over the railway to the left to reach the A55. Go right into Conwy.

(1) *Conwy*

The Romans had an interest in Conwy, having found that the oyster beds at Penarth, about 1.5 km (1 mile) downriver, yielded excellent pearls (Julius Caesar's breastplate was reputedly set with British pearls), but the first recorded dwellers on the present town site were Cistercian monks. At that stage the castle at the Afon Conwy's mouth was on the eastern bank, at Deganwy, but Edward I realised the tremendous importance of the river as a natural defence – an English soldier noted during an earlier campaign that, although the Welsh across the river were 'but a crossbow-shot' away, it might as well have been miles – and decided to build a fortified town. The monks were moved to Llanrwst, and the castle and town walls were built, in the amazing time of four years, for the equally amazing sum of £15 000 (about £6 million in present terms). In 1944 Sir Goronwy Edwards said that 'taken as a whole, Conwy is incomparably the most magnificent of Edward I's Welsh fortresses', and I see no reason at all to challenge so eminent an opinion. The visitor should walk around the walls – they are about a mile in length with three main gates and 21 defensive towers – and should not miss the castle which, though of a straightforward design, is almost complete and commands a marvellous position. The castle was sited on the river so that a siege could be withstood indefinitely, but in 1294 Edward I himself was besieged by Welsh rebels, and the castle's provisions decreased alarmingly as floodwaters on the river prevented ships from reaching the site. Eventually the waters receded and the king and his retinue celebrated a late Christmas, part of the festivities at this most joyous of Christian occasions being the execution of several Welsh bards believed, almost certainly wrongly, to have been behind the rebellion.

Near the castle, Thomas Telford's suspension bridge, designed to look like a drawbridge, is an excellent piece of engineering, as is Robert Stephenson's railway bridge beside it, even if they do detract from the view across the river of the castle.

Aberconwy House, on the corner of Castle Street and High Street, is the town's oldest house, dating from the fifteenth century. It is an elegant, elaborate house, now owned by the National Trust and housing an exhibition on Conwy's history.

(2) *Sychnant Pass*

Sychnant means dry valley, a very good description of the pass, but not one that suggests its elegance or beauty. The valley is also occasionally known as Echo Valley, though I confess ignorance of any particular reason for this.

Before the coast road from Conwy to Penmaenmawr was completed, the pass was the main route between the towns. So bad was the state of the pass on occasions that not only did the passengers in the coaches have to get out and walk, the effort of pulling being too great for the horses, but more than once the coach had to be partially dismantled and carried up the hill by the passengers!

(3) *Castell Caer Leion*

The name is, in part, Roman, though the earliest fortifications on
the hill are certainly pre-Roman Celtic. The ramparts of the fort,
built of stone in parts, are still 3.5 m (11½ ft) thick in places. The
ramparts do not include the northern side, where the natural slope
of the hill provides adequate defence. Inside the fort the remains of
more than 50 hut circles have been found.

From the hilltop, there are fine views of Anglesey and Conwy
town, and clear days reveal the Isle of Man and the hills of the Lake
District.

Walk 20   The Front Ridge of the Carneddau

Of the fourteen Welsh peaks – all in Snowdonia – that are more
than 3000 ft high, six lie in the Carneddau. Three of these lie on a
high ridge that extends from the top of Nant Ffancon almost all the
way along the Ogwen valley to Capel Curig. This walk takes that
ridge, which fronts the visitor who arrives along the A5. It is a
magnificent walk, with interest being maintained along its length,
and offering fine views, especially of the Glyders.

Walk category: Difficult (6 hours).

Length: 20 km (12½ miles) for full round trip.

Ascent: 1000 m (3300 ft).

Maps: Landranger Sheet 115; Outdoor Leisure Sheets 16 and 17.

Starting and finishing point: Car-parks and lay-bys near the Ogwen
Cottage at 650 603. An alternative to the full trip is to descend from
Pen Llithrig y Wrach, the final peak, to Capel Curig and to return
then by bus to the start. The bus service along the Ogwen valley is
not wonderful, however, and the short section of A5 on the full trip
is quite safe.

Sychnant Pass

Walk 20: The Front Ridge of the Carneddau

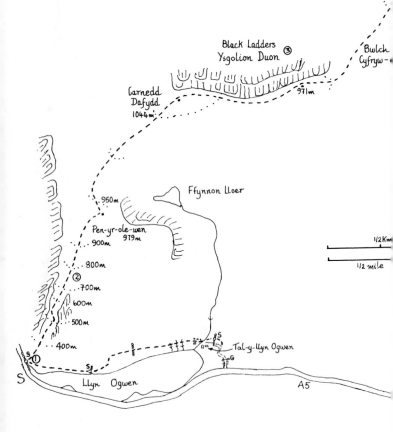

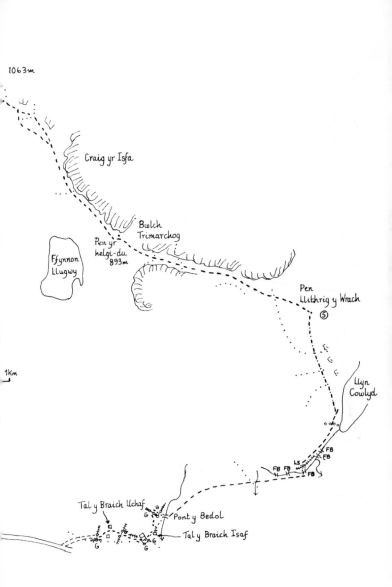

1063m

Craig yr Isfa

Bwlch
Trimarchog

Pen yr
helgi-du
893m

Ffynnon
Llugwy

Pen
Llithrig y Wrach
⑤

1Km

Llyn
Cowlyd

FB
FB
LS
FB
FB
FB
FB

Tal y Braich Uchaf
G
G
Pont y Bedol
G
G
Tal y Braich Isaf
G
G

Go along the A5 towards Bethesda to the stile, right, just beyond the bridge over the Afon Ogwen (see (1) The Alf Embleton stile). Over the stile a path climbs Pen-yr-ole-wen (see (2) Pen-yr-ole-wen).

After the gruelling climb, a fine ridge walk leads to Carnedd Dafydd, continuing along the edge of Ysgolion Duon (see (3) Ysgolion Duon, the Black Ladders) to the start of Bwlch Cyfryw-drum, the pass to Carnedd Llywelyn. Here, a ridge continues south-east falling to the Ffynnon Llugwy Reservoir, but the obvious way is over the pass, a delightfully narrow saddle with excellent views to each side, and on to Carnedd Llywelyn (see (4) The Carneddau).

Carnedd Llywelyn is the meeting point of four ridges running, more or less, along the cardinal point directions. We have come up the south ridge, and leave by going down the east ridge. As we descend, we drop below 3000 ft for the first time since we passed that contour on the climb to Pen-yr-ole-wen, 6 km (3¾ miles) ago.

The next point on the ridge is Craig yr Isfa, which is little more than a sharp 'pinnacle' on the ridge up to Pen yr helgi-du. From the summit there is a fine view of Ffynnon Llugwy, and an easy escape can be made from the summit down the CEGB's tarmacked road to the lake. No comment on the building of this road across a fine section of National Park is needed.

We go east down a very fine ridge to Bwlch Trimarchog, the whole length of the ridge commanding marvellous views into Cwm Eigiau, as well as, of course, the Glyders. The last rise is to Pen Llithrig y Wrach (see (5) the Eastern Peaks) from which a descent southwards reaches a path that follows Llyn Cowlyd's northern shore. From the tip of Llyn Cowlyd the path follows a drainage leat carrying water from the hillside into the reservoir. A footbridge over the leat is reached and ignored, the second bridge being taken to a path on the other side of the leat. At the second bridge from the one crossed the leat bends right, but we go left on a path to a delightful clapper bridge, Pont y Bedol.

Pen-yr-ole-wen from Cwm Idwal

Go over the bridge, through the fence gate and go ahead with a wall to your left hand for 50 m to a gateway, left. Through it a messy track leads to Tal y Braich Isaf farm. Beyond the gate at the last farm building go right along a raised ditch edge to a gate. Ahead now is more messy ground to Tal y Braich Uchaf, from where the A5 is reached straightforwardly. An apparently acceptable, but not a legitimate right-of-way, alternative to this unsatisfactory route is to go about 250 m rather than 50 m beyond Pont y Bedol. There go over the ladder stile and along a path above Tal y Braich Uchaf farm, that curves around the farm to join the track from it to the A5.

The edge can be taken off a walk along the A5 by going along the signed path to Tal-y-llyn Ogwen (667 608) from where a path along the northern shore of Llyn Ogwen returns to the start point.

(1) *The Alf Embleton stile*
The stile commemorates a famous treasurer of the Ramblers' Association and is discreetly engraved. A fine memorial.

(2) *Pen-yr-ole-wen*
The climb of Pen-yr-ole-wen, at a gradient of about 1 in 2 for nearly 700 m (2300 ft) to the first, false, summit, is the longest consistently steep climb in Wales. In places the going is difficult with hard, shiny earth littered with pebbles – reminiscent of ball-bearings on a steel plate – and it is necessary to repeat constantly that the Carneddau are a series of grassy whalebacks!

(3) *Ysgolion Duon, the Black Ladders*
Although too broken to be a first-rate rock-climbing crag, this delightfully named cliff is one of the foremost Welsh ice-climbing centres.

(4) *The Carneddau*
Carnedd Llywelyn and Carnedd Dafydd are named for the last two princes of the royal house of Gwynedd, Llywelyn the Last, killed near Brecon, and Dafydd, his brother, ignominiously executed as a traitor. Why these two peaks should be so named, rather than more distinctive ones, I do not know. Carnedd Llywelyn has the added

Carnedd Llywelyn and Yr Elen from Bwlch Cyfryw-drum

attraction of being one of the nineteen Holy Mountains in the world, according to an obscure sect in Los Angeles.

(5) *The Eastern Peaks*

Pen Lithrig y Wrach is the Hill of the Slippery Witch, and it can, with the right veil of mist, look like a crouched figure. Bwlch Trimarchog is the Pass of the Three Riders, Pen yr helgi-du is the Hill of the Black Dog. One of the great joys of walking in Wales is the thread of mystery that weaves its way among the peaks.

Walk 21   Two Lakes

The Conwy valley side of the Carneddau has a number of long valleys, most of which have lakes. We here explore two of these in the lower lying valleys to the south of the high peaks.

Walk category: Easy (2¼ hours).

Length: 9 km (5¾ miles).

Ascent: 150 m (500 ft).

Maps: Landranger Sheet 115; Outdoor Leisure Sheet 16.

Starting and finishing point: The car-park at 763 605 near the southern tip of Llyn Geirionydd, reached from the road on the west side of the Conwy valley, between Llanrwst and Trefriw.

From the car-park go left (south) to the tip of the lake (see (1) Llyn Geirionydd). There, where the road goes sharply left, go right on a track along the lake's tip. The track bears left and after 250 m a narrow but distinct path right goes steeply up into the forest.

The path crosses this first forest road twice and emerges from the forest where there is a meeting of several forest roads. Go ahead on the road that continues the direction of the path, but as this road

Pen Llithrig y Wrach from Pont Bedol

Walk 21: Two Lakes

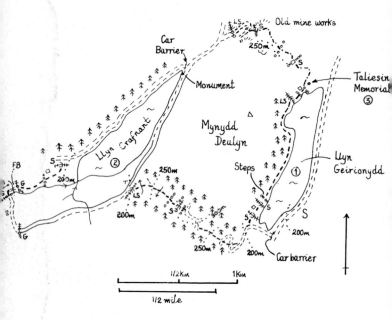

goes right, go half-left on a narrower stony path. In this area there are fine panoramic views to Moel Siabod, and to the Conwy valley.

The narrow path is followed downhill and, as it nears the valley bottom, at a Y-junction of paths, go left and over a stile to a metalled lane with a telephone box to the right. Follow the lane as it rises gently away from Llyn Crafnant, to its end at a gate. Go through the gate and turn right along a track past a wooden building

Llyn Geirionydd from the Taliesin Memorial

to almost reach Hendre. Just before it, however, between two gates go right over a footbridge on a path towards the lake. The path is obvious, using a stile to gain a forest track that leads to Llyn Crafnant, and closely follows its northern shore to its northern tip. (See (2) Llyn Crafnant.) Cross the lake's outfall stream to reach a lane. Go left and follow this for about 500 m to a forestry road going right (east).

Follow the road to a very sharp right bend where a path goes off left. The path crosses a stile to reach old mine workings to the right. *The workings are not considered safe and should not be entered.* At a fork in the path go right to continue around the ridge through a gap in one wall and over a stile at another, with a small piece of woodland between them. About 100 m from the second wall, go right at a junction of paths, along the grass track. Soon Llyn Geirionydd comes into view, as does a large cairn (see (3) Taliesin Memorial).

From the cairn go down to the lakeside and follow the path that goes all the way along the western shore to reach the outward route. Reverse that to the car-park.

(1) *Llyn Geirionydd*
The western shore of Llyn Geirionydd, though afforested, still bears visible signs of the lead mining carried on there. The lake's waters are extremely clear, but this is no indication of freedom from pollution, just another effect of the lead mining. The wash from the spoil has poisoned the lake with lead, so that little plant life grows in it.

(2) *Llyn Crafnant*
Llyn Crafnant is a reservoir supplying the Conwy valley, but shows little sign of it. The lake is magnificently situated in a long, broad cwm, and when viewed along its length is quite beautiful. Clogwyn yr Eryr, a stark cliff on the cwm's headwall, is a 'modern' cliff, covered in bold climbs.

The monument at Crafnant's northern tip records the gift of the lake to the people of the valley by Richard James Esq.

Llyn Crafnant

(3) *Taliesin Memorial*

Taliesin is a famed sixth-century Welsh poet known from sources
dating from about AD 1000, and from a collection of work, thought
to be chiefly if not exclusively the writings of one man, called the
Book of Taliesin. The bard is believed to have lived near the
northern end of Llyn Geirionydd.

Walk 22   The Gwydr Forest

If the Carneddau region is defined as the area between the A5 and
the Conwy valley – as it is here – then it also includes a section of the
Gwydr Forest and of the Llugwy valley. The valleys of the Afon
Llugwy and Afon Lledr that flow into the Conwy river near
Betws-y-Coed are two of the outstandingly attractive river valleys of
Wales. This walk follows the Afon Llugwy past the Swallow Falls,
Snowdonia's most famous waterfall, returning through the Gwydr
Forest. Some care is needed on the route, as the Forestry
Commission have a habit of driving new forestry roads that alter
route descriptions at a stroke.

Walk category: Easy (1¼ hours).

Length: 5 km (3 miles).

Ascent: 80 m (260 ft).

Maps: Landranger Sheet 115; Outdoor Leisure Sheet 16.

Starting and finishing point: The car-park, so called by the Forestry
Commission though it is neither large nor surfaced, at 758 577,
reached from the A5 by turning north off the A5 – that is, right if
approaching from Betws-y-Coed, left if approaching from Capel
Curig – at Ty-hyll, the Ugly House. The car-park is about 200 m
from the house, just beyond The Towers centre.

Walk 22 : The Gwydr Forest

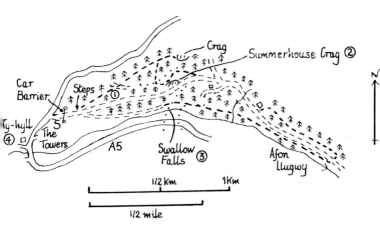

From the car-park a forest road leads off into the Gwydr Forest.
From it, after a short distance, steps go left, climbing steeply –
follow the yellow arrows – through a good section of mixed
woodland (see (1) Gwydr Forest) to a high-set crag, returning a few
metres from it to a yellow-arrowed path descending more gently
towards the top of Summerhouse Crag (see (2) Summerhouse
Crag). Beyond, the path descends again, to join a forest road. Go
left to join a metalled road. Here go right, passing another forest
road right, that can be taken to reduce the mileage, and continuing
for about 300 m. There just after the house, leave the road by steps
to the left.

The steps gain a path through the forest that rejoins the road
about 800 m further along. Go over the road to a path, and go right
along it.

The path offers superb views of the river – not least where the
river tumbles down the Swallow Falls (see (3) Swallow Falls). From

the falls a forest road leads easily back to the car park, though it is also possible to follow the river to the road at Ty-hyll (see (4) Ty-hyll, the Ugly House).

(1) *Gwydr Forest*

The Forestry Commission has made strenuous efforts in the Gwydr Forest to reduce the boredom and sterility of endless rows of conifers, and to make the area accessible. The early stages of the walk pass through good mixed woodland with oak, birch, beech, even horse and sweet chestnut, among the Japanese larch, Douglas fir and Norwegian spruce. Further on the forest is mainly western red cedar, but look out for several redwoods, giant sequoias, with their oddly fibrous bark.

(2) *Summerhouse Crag*

The crag is named for a summerhouse built in Victorian times to take advantage of the fine view, now over the forest, to Moel Siabod. If you have children please be careful: the crag's edge is abrupt and not well guarded.

(3) *Swallow Falls*

Swallow is an Anglicisation of the Welsh *ewynnol*, foaming, and in Welsh the falls are actually called Rhaeadr y Wennol. Again George Borrow – who was so delighted with the falls that he gave his Welsh guide sixpence, a small fortune at the time – gives an excellent decription: 'Two beautiful rolls of white water, dashing into a pool . . . then there is a swirl of water . . . into a pool black as death and seemingly of great depth; then a rush through a very narrow outlet into another pool, from which the water clamours away down the glen'.

   The pool is said to contain the soul of Sir John Gwynne of Gwydir, a man so evil that his soul was trapped to be purified by the water.

(4) *Ty-hyll, the Ugly House*

The house was built without mortar, and is a jumble of huge blocks. The reason for this lies in the date of its building, the fifteenth century, when the law stated that any free man who could, starting

at dawn, build a fireplace and chimney and have smoke rising by
dusk of the same day, had the rights over the land his new house
stood on and an parcel of land besides. The house itself could be
completed at the new owner's leisure. Beauty, and its absence, are
in the eye of the beholder, though, and I remain to be convinced
that the house is any uglier than many hundred other buildings.

MOEL SIABOD AND MOELWYNION

In an area bordered by Nantgwynant and the Llugwy valley to the
north, the Lledr valley and Vale of Ffestiniog to the south, and the
Afon Glaslyn to the west, is some very fine walking country. The
High peaks include Moel Siabod, famous among all who visit North
Wales by way of the A5, as its elegant lines dominate the last lap of
the route from Betws-y-Coed to Capel Curig.

The Moelwyns, Mawr and Bach, are shapely peaks standing over
the slate village of Blaenau Ffestiniog, and near them is Cnicht,
probably the most distinctive of all Welsh peaks – except, perhaps,
Tryfan – but only if viewed from the right direction, as we shall see.

To the west of our area streams drain the high land into the Afon
Glaslyn. This high land, between Cnicht and Moel Siabod, is for the
connoisseur, a twisted landscape of rock ridges and small lakes,
while the streams have carved valleys that are for the lover of fine
lowland scenery. Go to Nantmor where there is a fine forest walk,
but better, go to the valley of the Afon Glaslyn itself, where the
Aberglaslyn Pass is the most classically beautiful place that we shall
visit on any of our walks.

Walk 23   Moel Siabod

Moel Siabod is a beautiful peak when viewed from the A5 north of
Betws-y-Coed, but it is also a deceptive one. From that viewpoint it
is shapely, apparently the classical pyramid, whereas in fact it has a
long ridge and a surprisingly steep south-eastern face, which is well
seen from the suggested route.

Walk category: Intermediate (3½ hours).

Length: 10 km (6¼ miles).

Ascent: 750 m (2450 ft).

Maps: Landranger Sheet 115; Outdoor Leisure Sheet 16.

Starting and finishing point: The lay-by on the A5 at 735 571, about 1.5 km (1 mile) south of Capel Curig.

From the lay-by go towards Capel Curig, pausing almost before you have set off to view the Cyfyng Falls on the Afon Llugwy. These falls need heavy rain to be truly spectacular, but are good nonetheless. A few metres further on, go left over Pont Cynfyg. Ignore a signed footpath right after a few metres for another, also right, about 100 m from the bridge which follows a steep farm road to Rhôs farm.

A track continues from the farm over a stile to a junction of paths. Here take the right fork, the left fork leading to an old quarry (see (1) Capel Curig Slate Quarries). The path crosses a second ladder stile and goes on to a pair of ladder stiles. The right one leads to a direct route to Moel Siabod, so take the left one to a path that goes beside a lake and on to an old quarry filled with water. The ruined buildings beside the quarry are very dilapidated and should not be entered. The quarry pit should also not be entered. The water looks far from inviting, the sort of place around which legends grow up.

The path skirts the left side of the quarry and heads off to the slight col between the huge wall of Moel Siabod to the right and a grassy hillock to the left. When this is reached the lake of Llyn y Foel comes into view, lying slightly below the walker (see (2) Llyn y Foel). Go along the lake's northern shore continuing to the obvious ridge of Daiar Ddu which is followed to the summit of Moel Siabod (see (3) Moel Siabod). There is a path up the ridge, which offers the occasional piece of limited scrambling.

Walk 23 : Moel Siabod

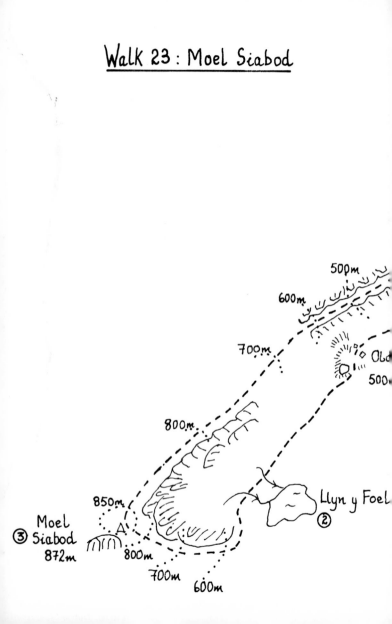

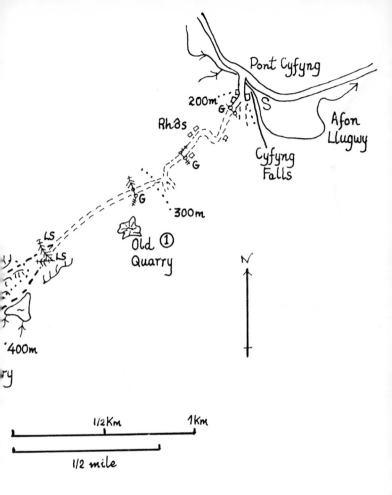

Pont Cyfyng

200m

G

Rhôs

G

Afon
Llugwy

Cyfyng
Falls

300m

LS

Old ① Quarry

LS

G

N

400m

ry

1/2 Km   1 Km

1/2 mile

From the summit triangulation pillar go north-east, to the long ridge above the steep south-eastern face that is such a deceptive feature of Moel Siabod. The path is distinct and leads to the outward route at the third ladder stile. From there, the outward journey is reversed.

(1) *Capel Curig Slate Quarries*
A company was formed in the nineteenth century to work slate in several places on the flank of Moel Siabod, one effect of the workings being the quarrying of the huge water-filled pit passed on the outward journey. Transport difficulties and the poor quality of the slate meant that the works were never very profitable, and by the early twentieth century the quarries had closed.

(2) *Llyn y Foel*
The lake is an excellent example of a glacially formed corrie lake. The imposing south-east face of Moel Siabod and the ridge of Daiar Ddu set the lake in a rugged and wild cwm which is also rarely frequented – a real find for the wilderness seeker. Interestingly, from a position that is only a little way above the lake, the 'friendly' delights of the Lledr valley can be viewed, including an excellent sight of the remains of Dolwyddelan Castle.

(3) *Moel Siabod*
Because of its isolation, the peak commands a magnificent panorama taking in most of the hill ranges of northern Snowdonia. The view of the Snowdon Horseshoe is especially fine.

Walk 24   Llyn Dinas and the Aberglaslyn Pass

This walk traverses the Aberglaslyn Pass, the most famous, and justly so, of Snowdonia's gorges, as well as visiting the grave of the legendary Gelert, and a spot associated with the most renowned of Celtic magicians. A magnificent walk, not to be missed.

Moel Siabod from Summerhouse Crag on Walk 22

Walk category: Easy (2½ hours).

Length: 9.5 km (6 miles).

Ascent: 250 m (800 ft).

Maps: Landranger Sheet 115; Outdoor Leisure Sheet 16 and 17.

Starting and finishing point: Car-parks in Beddgelert village.

From wherever your car is parked, reach the southern side – the side furthest from the roads to Caernarfon and Capel Curig, closest to Porthmadog – of the main Beddgelert bridge (see (1) Beddgelert). Here go east, away from the Porthmadog road, with the river on your left hand, along a minor road. Go over a bridge and bear left along the river bank. At a second bridge do not cross, but continue with the river still on your left hand, though further away. Go over a ladder stile and on to a gate to a road. Go right, to follow the road to its end at a gate. Go through the gate and left on to a lane past Ty-hên. Go left with the wall to a bridge. To the right here is the Sygun mine (see (2) Sygun mine). Do not cross the bridge but go on, passing fine rhododendron trees and Cae'r-moch (right), to a gate. Go through and follow the lane past another bridge to reach Llyn Dinas. The Dinas of the name is the prominent tree-covered mound that has been visible across the river for the last few hundred metres of the walk (see (3) Dinas Emrys).
  At the tip of Llyn Dinas two paths meet. The left one takes the southern shoreline of the lake, but we go right on a path that zigzags up the hillside to reach a prominent rock outcrop at Bwlch y Sygyn.
  From the pass take an indistinct track going south – soon passing a small pool – to reach a wider, more distinct path. Follow this down Cwm Bychan passing, at several places, old spoil heaps and even the rusting remains of an aerial ropeway, reminders of mining. The path crosses a stream, goes through a gate and emerges on an old railway track (see (4) Welsh Highland Railway). The easy way now is to go right, through the tunnel which is quite safe and free of large holes, though it can be damp and has the odd stone to trip the

walker. Alternatively, go across the track and down through fine woodland to Pont Aberglaslyn, going right there *before* the road on an adventurous path beside the river, rising to meet the railway track beyond the tunnel. The alternative route does capture the best of Aberglaslyn's scenery, and with its steps and wooden bridges is an excellent outing. (See (5) Aberglaslyn Pass).

Follow the railway – there are other, much shorter tunnels for the tunnel enthusiast – until it crosses a bridge, beyond which go right on a distinct path that is followed back to Beddgelert, with one short detour left to visit the famous grave (see (6) Gelert's grave).

(1) *Beddgelert*

Beddgelert is a pretty village, famous beyond its capacity to absorb summer visitors with whom it can be choked. The walk described is excellent when springtime flowers are first blooming and when autumn gives a copper colour to the trees of Aberglaslyn and the bracken near the copper mines. If you have no alternative but to visit in summer, try the walk very early or very late.

It is probable that only the monastery of Bardsey Island was earlier than an Augustinian priory built at Beddgelert. The house probably existed in one form or another – possibly in its earliest form as a simple hermit's cell – as early as the sixth century. Today, the flat field below the church, on the west side of the Afon Glaslyn, is all that remains of the priory, though the church itself, which was the priory church, does have some original features. Chief of these are the three elegant windows in the east wall. Unfortunately the church suffered badly from Victorian 'restorers'.

(2) *Sygun mine*

Although no mining is recorded here before 1825 it is likely that the site is more ancient, there even being a tradition of Roman mines. The workings at Sygun were by adit, that is a shaft driven horizontally into the hill rather than vertically. The advantage of this was that a slight gradient on the shaft allowed water to drain naturally – vertical shafts needed pumping power to remove their water – and the men could walk in, rather than needing expensive and time-consuming lift cages. Early discoveries at the mine were very promising (though whether they were ever quite as promising as the advertising for the share issues suggested is debatable) but the promise, as so often in North Wales, was not realised and the mine limped from crisis to crisis until its eventual closure early this century. Today it is a thriving tourist attraction.

In Cwm Bychan, the mining was by vertical shafts. High up towards Bwlch y Sygyn the aerial ropeway took buckets of ore to a, still intact, dressing plant near the bottom of the cwm. The rusting ropeway towers seem less obtrusive than electricity transmission lines – will someone, some day, extol the virtues of decaying pylons? – and those patient and lucky enough may still find an ore bucket hidden in the bracken.

(3) *Dinas Emrys*

Dinas Emrys is the legendary home of Vortigern, the Celtic king who invited the Saxons into Kent. The hill does have some Celtic and early medieval fortifications, but it is as Vortigern's fortress that it holds the imagination. It is said that when workmen were building the king's castle they returned to the site each morning to discover that the previous day's work had been swallowed up by the earth. Vortigern's magicians told him he must sacrifice a boy with no father at the site to remove the evil that was destroying the work. The king's messengers eventually found such a boy, son of a royal princess but fathered by a half-man half-angel, a Greek-type demi-god.

The boy was taken to the site where, before he could be sacrificed, he accused Vortigern's magicians of false prophecy, claiming that the castle disappeared each night into an underground pool that had to be drained before a castle could be completed. Workmen dug, found the pool and drained it to reveal two sleeping dragons, one red and one white, who awoke to fight, first one having the upper claw then the other, neither ever gaining a winning advantage.

The boy was Merlin, later Arthur's magician, and the dragons were believed to foretell the battles between the Celts and the Saxons and, later, the Welsh (the Red Dragon) and the Normans. Interestingly, in another story, in the *Mabinogion*, a collection of

Ruined Ropeway in Cwm Bychan, Beddgelert

early Celtic legends, Lludd, king of Britain, is said to have buried red and white dragons in Snowdonia to rid the country of a plague of screaming.

(4) *Welsh Highland Railway*

This line, which ran for 35 km (22 miles) from Porthmadog to Dinas Junction, Caernarfon, was the longest narrow-gauge line in Wales. It started as a 5 km (3 mile) section taking visitors from Caernarfon to South Snowdon station at Rhyd-ddu, from where they could walk to Snowdon's summit. This line, completed in 1881, was very successful until the Snowdon Mountain Railway opened in 1896, when it went into decline and was eventually forced to close due to lack of custom. Only in the first quarter of this century was the line to Porthmadog completed. This was a bold move for the time – the car was rapidly replacing rail transport – and deserved to succeed, but it did not, and the line closed in 1937. Recently the line has been bought, and a 1.25 km (¾ mile) section at Porthmadog has been opened. The owners hope, eventually, to re-open the line to Beddgelert.

(5) *Aberglaslyn Pass*

An eighteenth-century visitor to the pass wrote: 'How shall I express my feelings! The dark tremendous precipices, the rapid river roaring over disjointed rocks, black caverns, and issuing cataracts; all serve to make this the noblest specimen of the Finely Horrid the eye can possibly behold; the Poet has not described, nor the Painter pictured so gloomy a retreat, 'tis the last approach to the mansion of Pluto through the regions of Despair.' What can be made of such sentiments? Did he believe this, or was it written for readers who wanted to be thrilled? We come to see all those natural features seeking not horror but beauty, and finding it in good measure.

The name Aberglaslyn means Confluence of the Blue Lake, *aber* meaning confluence rather than mouth as it is usually translated. True, it usually means mouth, i.e. confluence of river and sea, but that meaning goes sadly wrong at Abergavenny. Here, though, the river of the blue lake did meet the sea: nearby Nantmor was

Aberglaslyn Pass

Nant-y-mor, the Valley of the Sea, and ships sailed to Pont Aberglaslyn. All this changed when William Madocks built his cob at Porthmadog in the early nineteenth century, reclaiming the estuary, making the sea cliffs of Tremadog an inland crag, and placing Aberglaslyn nearly 8 km (5 miles) from its *aber*.

(6) *Gelert's grave*

The story is that Llywelyn the Great had a faithful hunting dog, Gelert, who was left at home one day to guard the prince's baby son. A wolf came into the nursery and Gelert fought it to save the boy, killing it but being hurt in doing so, and overturning the boy's cradle. When Llywelyn came home he saw bloodstained blankets and cradle, and a bloodstained Gelert. Assuming the dog had killed the boy he drew his sword and killed Gelert, whose dying yelp awoke the boy asleep under the blankets. Llywelyn pulled back the blankets to reach the crying boy and found, also, the dead wolf. Overcome with remorse the prince buried the dog under a fine cairn. That is the grave we see here, which also gives a name to the village, Beddgelert, the Grave of Gelert.

The story is excellent, but the original version is in Sanskrit, and in Welsh it precedes Llywelyn, though it is possible it was transferred to him because his father-in-law, King John, is known to have given him a deer-hunting dog called Killhart.

The real story begins much, much later with David Pritchard, late eighteenth-century owner of Beddgelert's Royal Goat Hotel, who re-invented the story to bring in some welcome trade. The best comment on the episode is in verse:

> Pass on O tender hearted, dry your eyes;
> Not here a greyhound, but a landlord lies.

The village's name probably derives from an early Celtic saint, perhaps the first hermit, called Celert or Celei. There was also once an Irish chieftain who lived near the village and his name may have been Celert.

Walk 25   Cnicht

This is the best 'first mountain' in Wales – a straightforward walk
with limited climbing in terms of feet ascended, up one of the most
elegant of Welsh mountains.

Walk category: Easy (2¼ hours).

Length: 6 km (3¾ miles).

Ascent: 550 m (1800 ft).

Maps: Landranger Sheets 115 and 124; Outdoor Leisure Sheet 19.

Starting and finishing point: The car-park at 631 447 in Croesor
village.

From the car-park go right, through Croesor village (see (1)
Croesor), going ahead at the crossroads. To the right, just beyond
the helpful vandalism – 'Cnicht' inscribed on the slate wall – is an
epic memorial to Bob Owen Croesor (see (2) Bob Owen Croesor).
The lane rises, falls, and rises again and reaches a gate. Beyond is a
junction of paths: the path ahead is to Nantmor, so go right on the
signed path, passing a ruined building to a ladder stile. Beyond, the
path is both distinct and well signed until the narrow summit ridge
of Cnicht is reached. Go up, occasionally steeply, but always with
very fine positions, to the summit (see (3) Cnicht). Return by the
same route.

(1) *Croesor*
Near the village is Ffynnon Helen, Helen's Spring, named for the
same Princess Elin who gave her name to Sarn Helen (see
Introduction to Snowdonia). Legend has it that once on a journey
from North to South Wales the princess stopped by the spring to
refresh herself while waiting for the second half of her party,
commanded by her son. As her son's party passed Castell Cidwm,
to the west of Snowdon, the giant Cidwm, after whom the spot is

Walk 25 : Cnicht
Walk 26 : The Moelwyns

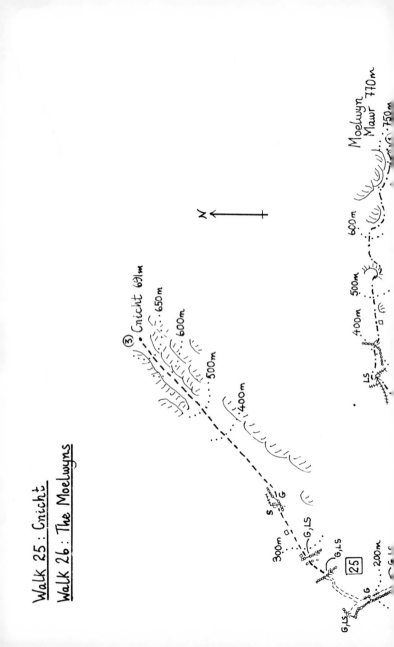

N

Cnicht 689m ③

650m

600m

500m

400m

300m

S
G

G,LS

G,LS

G,LS

25

200m

G,LS

G

400m 500m 600m

Moelwyn Mawr 770m
750m

LS

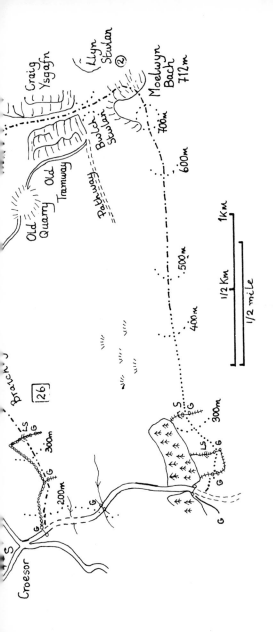

Croesor

S

Branch

26

Old Quarry

Old Tramway

Craig Ysgafn

Llyn Stwlan ②

Bwlch Stwlan

Pathway

Moelwyn Bach 712m

700m

600m

500m

400m

300m

Ls
G
300m
G
G
200m
S
G

S
G
300m
Ls
G
G

1Km

1/2 Km

1/2 mile

named, rushed out and attacked the party, killing the princess's son. An escaping member of the party hurried on to the spring and broke the sad news to the princess who cried out in despair, '*O, Croes awr*' – 'Oh, cursed hour.' From then on, this spot was known as Croesor.

(2) *Bob Owen Croesor*

Born in 1885, Bob Owen had a 'traditional' Welsh upbringing, poor, wet and cold, followed by 30 years as clerk in the local quarry, an employment that ceased one Saturday when, with no notice at all, the quarry closed. Despite these setbacks, Bob became a recognised expert on aspects of Welsh history, with a self-amassed library that, by the time of his death in 1962, was around 50 000 volumes. He was given an honorary degree by the University of Wales in 1931, and in the late 1940s made many radio broadcasts, appeared on television and became a minor celebrity.

(3) *Cnicht*

Though often called the Welsh Matterhorn, the mountain has an English name, Cnicht being derived from *cnight*, the Old English word for a knight's fighting helmet. The name is believed to have been given to the peak by sailors in Cardigan Bay who used its distinctive helmet shape as a landmark. It is a low peak – 690 m (2264 ft) – but extremely elegant when viewed from the west. At the summit it is seen that the peak is only the western high spot of a long ridge. From Llyn Dinas this ridge is seen in profile and it can be difficult to reconcile the two hugely different views.

Walk 26   The Moelwyns

To the right of Cnicht, when it is viewed from the west, are the shapely masses of the two Moelwyn peaks. The peaks are also seen to good effect from the A470 Dolgellau-Porthmadog road. On a straight section near Trawsfynydd, the peaks rear up above the Vale of Ffestiniog, the Llyn Stwlan dam-wall showing like the white, grinning teeth in a dark skull. Occasionally the dam is floodlit at night, giving a surreal aspect to the hills.

Cnicht

Walk category: Intermediate (3¾ hours).

Length: 9 km (5¾ miles).

Ascent: 750 m (2500 ft).

Maps: Landranger Sheets 115 and 124; Outdoor Leisure Sheet 19.

Starting and finishing point: The car-park at Croesor, as Walk 25.

From the car-park at Croesor (see note (1) of Walk 25) go left along the lane. Go ahead at a crossroads, and follow the road to a gate. Beyond, go left, the road is unfenced, following the wall, and the indistinct path beyond it to gain Braich-y-Parc, the wonderful crescent-shaped ridge that leads to the summit of Moelwyn Mawr. Near the top, Braich-y-Parc is marred by close-range views of quarry ruins, but as a continuous gentle ridge it has few equals in Wales. Also in the latter stages a pair of rock towers need turning – go, with surprising ease, to the right.

The summit has an Ordnance Survey triangulation pillar, and a tremendous panorama (see (1) Moelwyn views). From the summit the broken ridge to Moelwyn Bach is reached by going slightly east, then descending with care over Craig Ysgafn to Bwlch Stwlan. Escape is easy here down the obvious pathway that leads up to the quarry tramway. Unfortunately the pathway disappears into a bog near its lower end. The Moelwyns are unfrequented and lack distinct paths, so from Bwlch Stwlan bear left along a faint path among the scree to a grassed ridge to the north-east of the summit, and use this ridge to gain the top (see (2) Ffestiniog Power Station).

From Moelwyn Bach descend west down a long grassed ridge – do not attempt to go north, the basin of the Afon Maesgwn is very boggy – towards the fenced conifer stand. Go to the left of the wood, by way of gates, to gain the unfenced road. Go right, following the road back to Croesor.

The Moelwyns

(1) *Moelwyn views*

As with Moel Siabod, the isolated position of the Moelwyns means that the panoramas from the summits are especially fine. Apart from the northern Snowdonia ranges, Moelwyn Bach offers views southward to the Berwyns, Arenigs and Rhinogs, as well as across the reclaimed estuary of the Afon Glaslyn to Porthmadog.

(2) *Ffestiniog Power Station*

The power station that uses water from Llyn Stwlan is pumped-storage, operating exactly as that at Dinorwig (see note (3) of Walk 17). This station is much smaller, however, generating 300 megawatts of electrical power.

MOEL HEBOG

To the east of Snowdon the hills are lower, falling away to the Lleyn peninsula, but there is still the odd gem. Below we explore just such a gem, a magnificent ridge.

Walk 27   The Nantlle Ridge

To the south of the B4418 that links the A4085 at Rhyd-ddu to the A487 at Penygroes is a long jagged ridge. Our walk takes that ridge, a magnificent outing, arguably the finest long ridge in Wales after the Snowdon Horseshoe, and traversing some fine and interesting country.

Walk category: Difficult (4¾ hours).

Length: 12 km (7½ miles).

Ascent: 950 m (3100 ft).

Maps: Landranger Sheet 115; Outdoor Leisure Sheet 17.

Porthmadog from the mine ruin, Moelwyn Mawr

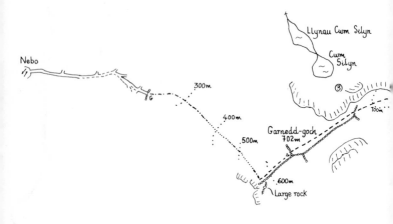

Llynau Cwm Silyn

Cwm
Silyn

Nebo

③

300m

400m

500m

700m

Garnedd-goch
702m

600m

Large rock

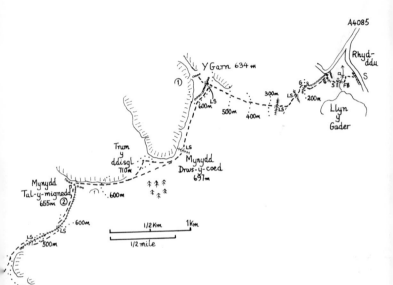

A4085

Rhyd-
ddu

Y Garn 634 m

①

600m   LS

300m

LS   S
FB
S

6

6

200m

Llyn
y
Gader

500m   400m

LS

Trum
y
ddisgl
710m   LS

Mynydd
Drws-y-coed
697m

Mynydd
Tal-y-mignedd
655m ②

①   600m

600m

LS   LS

300m

1/2 Km   1Km

1/2 mile

600m

Llyn
m

Starting and finishing point: The long ridge of Nantlle is not amenable to a round trip and the only reasonable walking route from the finishing point back to the starting point doubles the route mileage. The best solution is to use two cars, one being left at the finish point at Nebo (479 505), just off the A487 Porthmadog-Caernarfon road, the other returning to the start at Rhyd-ddu (569 529) on the A4085 Beddgelert-Caernarfon road. Another solution is to leave a car at Caernarfon, using the bus (Gwynedd Bus 11) to reach Rhyd-ddu (the journey takes around 40 minutes and buses are about hourly, but much less frequent on Sundays and Bank Holidays), returning to Caernarfon by bus from Nebo (this journey takes about 30 minutes on Gwynedd Bus 12, but there are only four services daily and none on Sundays – buses leave Nebo at 8.25, 10.45, 12.45 and 17.45).

There is a car-park in Rhyd-ddu, at 571 526. Reach that point and cross the A4085 to a gate and signed path, to the right, towards Llyn y Gader, a popular lake with anglers. The path reaches a bridge over a stream, but do not cross it. Instead go left to cross another bridge a few metres along, taking the path beyond to a farm track. Go right and down to a gate at the road. Do not go on to the road, but left through a gate to a path that follows the wall to the right to a gap in a fence. Go left along the fence, then ahead and over a ladder stile to an arrowed boulder. Here go right along a path that crosses a fence by ladder stile and continues to the summit of Nantlle Y Garn, the peak ahead with the distinctive, steep northern face.

From the summit, reached by ladder stile over a wall, there is a superb view of the western side of the Snowdon range, a side only seen from here as it is the eastern aspect that is featured on virtually all photographs of the range. From here, the view into Cwm Pennant (see (1) Cwm Pennant) is also excellent, and views into this fine cwm stay with us throughout the walk.

Follow the wall, keeping it to your right, southwards, keeping to the path when it ends; along the edge of some impressive cliffs. The last section of the ridge to the summit of Mynydd Drws-y-coed is

The first climb, to Nantlle Y Garn

quite exciting. From the summit follow the cliff edge round to Trum-y-ddisgl and from its top descend south-west along a grassed ridge to a slight col. From the col an obvious ridge rises to the west, again with cliffs to the right, and with one very narrow section, to reach the towering cairn on Mynydd Tal-y-mignedd's summit (see (2) Mynydd Tal-y-mignedd). From the summit a fence descends south-west. Follow this, crossing it twice by ladder stile, once near Bwlch Dros-bern, the obvious pass ahead, and once at the Bwlch. At the far side of the Bwlch, where the fence becomes a wall and reaches a rock outcrop, an indistinct path leads up a shattered ridge to the summit of Craig Cwm Silyn. The crag of the name lies below the summit, overlooking the twin lakes of Llynau Cwm Silyn (see (3) Craig Cwm Silyn). There is a fine view from here of Moel Hebog, the highest of the range's peaks (see (4) Moel Hebog).

Now go south-west to reach a wall and follow it to the summit of Garnedd-goch with its Ordnance Survey triangulation pillar. From there, continue along the wall running south-west, watching for a fence that starts on the other side of the wall, near an obvious large rock. There, go right, north-west, on an indistinct path that becomes more distinct as you descend. The path leads down progressively less steep ground to a wall, with a gate to a lane. Go into the lane, ignoring a gate right, to swing slightly right then left to a lane that leads to Nebo.

(1) *Cwm Pennant*

Cwm Pennant is one of the finest pastoral cwms in the National Park. Though famous for its industrial archaeology sites, it has been, in fact, little touched by the hand of man, and remains a farming valley. The high peaks of the Nantlle ridge to the north and west, and the high ridge from Moel Hebog to the east, all seeming much higher than their true height because of the low valley floor, crowd in on the cwm, giving it an enclosed, timeless feel. Cwm Pennant is a tranquil place, a place for peaceful contemplation. It is gloriously summed up by the rhetorical question of Eifion Wyn: 'Oh God, why didst Thou make Cwm Pennant so beautiful and the life of an old shepherd so short?'

For the industrial archaeologist there is much of interest. The old

Prince of Wales Slate Quarry at the head of the cwm was of
considerable importance and included a railway whose line can still
be traced to Porthmadog. Elsewhere, the most astonishing sight is
that of an old, but decaying, waterwheel (at 526 478) that once
supplied power to the copper mines of Cwm Ciprwrth. The wheel,
in cast iron, is 24 ft in diameter, 3½ ft wide, and still bears the
maker's tag – Dingey and Son, Truro.

(2) *Mynydd Tal-y-mignedd*

The cairn on the summit is all that remains of a tower built to
commemorate the Diamond Jubilee of Queen Victoria. The tower
is in a poor state of repair and has apparently been reduced in
height considerably in the years since the Second World War.

  The views from this early part of the ridge, into the Nantlle valley
and across it to Mynydd Mawr and Craig-y-bera, are excellent. The
quarries in the valley worked the Cambrian rock, and though not as
big as either Dinorwig or Penrhyn, Bethesda, were of considerable
importance.

(3) *Craig Cwm Silyn*

The great crag of Craig-yr-Ogof standing above the lakes has a long
history in Welsh rock climbing. The Great Slab is a fine sweep of
rock, 120 m (400 ft) long, that received early attention from Noel
Odell, the last person to see Mallory and Irvine alive on Everest, as
well as Colin Kirkus and Menlove Edwards.

(4) *Moel Hebog*

Moel Hebog is the Hill of the Falcon. In the eastern face of Moel yr
Ogof, the Hill of the Cave, beside it, are several large, horizontal
slots, and in the largest Owain Glyndŵr is said to have hidden.
During the last years of Glyndŵr's rebellion he became a fleeting
figure, his appearances shrouded in mystery. Some maintain he died
as early as 1406, the last years of the rebellion being sustained by
reference to a prince 'in hiding' who was actually long dead. Others
maintain that the pressures of the war, and despair at losing it,
caused him to lose his mind and that he spent his last years living as
a mad hermit in caves like this one. It can only be hoped that the
rebel did, in fact, find some peace, and died quietly.

THE RHINOGS

The wildest, most rugged country in North Wales is to be found in the long, but narrow, strip of upland that lies between the A470 Dolgellau-Maentwrog road and the sea. Geologically the Rhinogs are more normally called the Harlech Dome, for this is the upthrust dome of Cambrian rock spoken of in the introduction to the Snowdonia section. The softer sedimentary layers have weathered from the dome, to leave the hard, bare Rhinog grits of the Cambrian sub-strata. To the north of the range this hard, bare rock has produced a phenomenal country, difficult to cross, unrelenting and unforgiving. That area is also a nature reserve, and the walker is likely to plunge occasionally into vegetation the reserve seeks to protect. Our routes avoid the reserve, and deliberately so, the first route skirting the area on an ancient road, the others lying to the south.

It is fitting that we should take an ancient road here, because this is an ancient landscape. As we have seen, there are fine neolithic sites on the thin coastal plain between the peaks and Cardigan Bay. It is equally fitting that this range of hard, unyielding rock should once have protected a group of hard, unyielding outlaws. These, the bandits of Ardudwy, inhabited the coastal plain, protected by the high Rhinog ridge as well as any group were ever protected by a man-made wall. They would ride out occasionally to pillage the country beyond the ridge, always returning quickly to their lair. On one trip, it is said, they rode into Clwyd, kidnapping several local girls. On their return they were overtaken by the irate Clwyd menfolk who killed the bandits. The girls, overcome by grief at losing their romantic new lovers, drowned themselves in a nearby lake, still called to this day Llyn Morwynion, the Lake of the Maidens. The lake is to the east of Llan Ffestiniog.

Walk 28   The Bronze Age Road

This fine walk takes a route that was first trodden at least 3000 years ago, and when those Bronze Age traders came this way the land looked much as it does now. That is an amazing, and very

stimulating, thought to take with you on your traverse.
This route should not be attempted in poor visibility when the walker may become unnervingly lost, or after prolonged rain when he will certainly become very wet.

Walk category: Intermediate (4¼ hours).

Length: 18 km (11¼ miles).

Ascent: 200 m (660 ft).

Maps: Landranger Sheet 124; Outdoor Leisure Sheet 19.

Starting and finishing point: The route, a west to east traverse of the northern Rhinogs, is not amenable to a round trip. The alternative to being dropped and collected, or to using two cars, is to use buses. Both Harlech and Trawsfynydd are connected to the Oakley Arms, Maentwrog by bus – Harlech by Gwynedd Bus 38, Trawsfynydd by Gwynedd Bus 35. In each case the journey takes about 20 minutes. Each of the buses offers a reasonably frequent service, but Bus 35 does *not* operate on Sundays. The route given below assumes the walker will traverse from Harlech to Trawsfynydd, and the route length will be reduced if the walker is transported to the start of the walk and collected from the end.

From Harlech (see (1) Harlech) take the steep lane opposite the castle, and at the junction about 2 km (1¼ miles) along it, with a chapel and a telephone box at the near, right corner; turn left. From here we follow the Bronze Age road, marked at intervals by standing stones, the first of which we pass, to the right, after about 1 km (1100 yds). A second to the left is reached 500 m further on – after a road leading off right, signed 'Cwm Bychan', and a cattle grid are passed – while a third, a very small one, stands a little to the right of the road 450 m further on again.

About 400 m beyond the third stone, the lane bends left at a fourth. Here the ancient track continues as a green lane passing a sign reading 'No vehicle access. No parking'. About 100 m after

Walk 28: The Bronze Age Road (Western Section)

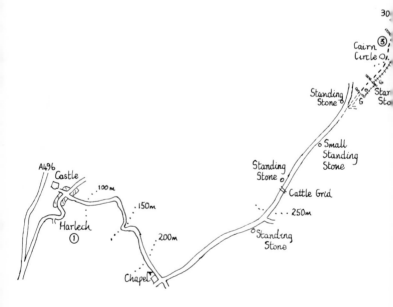

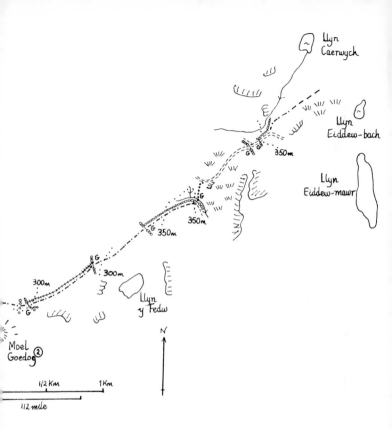

Llyn
Caerwych

Llyn
Eiddew-bach

350m

Llyn
Eiddew-mawr

G

350m

G   350m

350m

G

G   300m

300m

G

Llyn
y Fedw

N

Moel
Goedog ②

1/2 Km   1Km

1/2 mile

Walk 28 : The Bronze Age Road (Eastern Section)

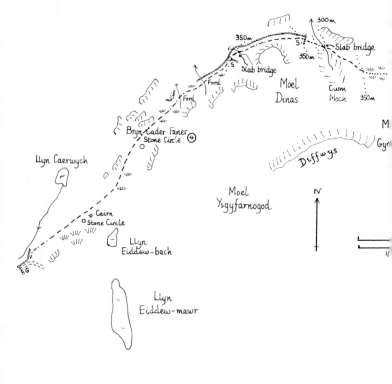

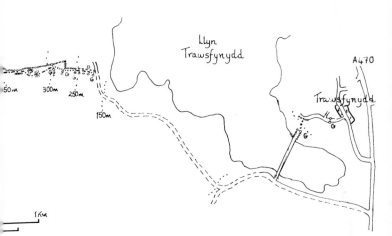

Llyn
Trawsfynydd

A470

Trawsfynydd

G

G

50m   300m   250m

150m

1 Km

leaving the lane, at a Y-junction of tracks, bear left to pass another standing stone before reaching a stone, technically a cairn, circle. The path now contours around Moel Goedog (see (2) Moel Goedog) before climbing across open country, with fine views northward (see (3) Northern View).

A wall is reached, and as this bears right to avoid an obvious bog ahead, a gate, left, gives access to very boggy ground. Follow a very indistinct path across this to a distinct track. Go right along this track, passing two gates. Beyond the second, the track follows a wall, but soon bears right away from it. Do not follow it, but instead go with the wall, then slightly right to join an indistinct, but obvious green track. A small stone circle is passed, right, and shortly after there is an ancient, now ruined, cairn, also right. Beyond, a ridge to the right is topped by the Bryn Cader Faner stone circle, a highlight of the walk (see (4) Bryn Cader Faner). To reach the circle it is necessary to leave the track.

Ahead now, following the path requires care. At some boggy patches it crosses by way of flat slabs, but at others it disappears, and must be relocated once the bog has been crossed. It is never devious however, so that its line is always fairly clear. Ultimately a wall gives the line – keep it at your left hand, avoiding the temptation to go through a gap at one point. Now the real beauty of the route can be savoured, as the walker is freed from the rigours of route-finding. As it contours around Moel Dinas, the track, that was later used as a coach route!, is at some points supported by rocks, at others it is lined with stones. At length a fence bars the way, a semi-stile – a stone assisted step-over – gives access to the magnificently wild Cwm Moch. A slab bridge is used to cross the stream, beyond which the track rises obviously to disappear in another bog.

Ahead a col is reached, and the view to Trawsfynydd lake and its power station opens up (see (5) Trawsfynydd Power Station). Go ahead to a gate in a wall, beyond which a path leads to a wall that is followed by an occasionally indistinct path downwards. At one point a solitary tree offers a change of scenery. Leave the wall as it

The Bryn Cader Faner stone circle beside the Bronze Age Road

reaches a fence, going right to a gate that leads to a path to the road along the lake's western edge.

Follow the road and just after passing a road joining from the right a barn on legs is reached. Here a ladder stile gives early access to the lake dam. The right-of-way is via a fenced path a little further along. Use the footbridge to cross the lake. At its end go ahead to reach a lane. Go right and into Trawsfynydd.

(1) *Harlech*
Harlech Castle is probably the most well-known of all the Edwardian castles of Wales, a tribute as much to the song 'Men of Harlech' as to the grandeur of its position, high on a rocky outcrop. When it was first built in 1283, to hold the coastal plain behind the Rhinogs, the sea lapped the foot of the cliff that supports the castle, the remains of a water gate still being visible. The castle has a very basic design, a square within a square, with corner towers and a ditch to further protect the landward sides. It saw real action only once, in the rebellion of Owain Glyndŵr when it was captured in 1404, after a long siege, by Owain and used as his headquarters and royal court until its recapture in early 1409. The retaking included a long bombardment by that new war engine, the cannon, which destroyed virtually the whole of the wall of the outer square. It was a later siege, in 1468 during the Wars of the Roses, that gave rise to the famous 'Men of Harlech'.

(2) *Moel Goedog*
The hill-fort on top of this peak is Iron Age rather than Bronze Age, evidence of the continued importance of the road. The fort is circular, about 250 m in diameter and protected on all sides by two series of ramparts and ditches. To the north there is a third series of defences. One interesting feature is the way that the inner rampart has utilised natural rock outcrops.

The Road in Cwm Moch

(3) *Northern View*

The view north over the estuary of the Afon Dwyryd is excellent, but the eye is drawn to what appears to be a village transplanted to here from Italy. This is Portmeirion, an architectural folly on a grand scale. It was conceived and constructed by Sir Clough Williams-Ellis in the second quarter of this century and has inspired and intrigued many a visitor in the years since then.

(4) *Bryn Cader Faner*

The stone circle here was the finest Bronze Age site in what was to become the Snowdonia National Park. It was constructed of about 30 stones which leaned outwards rather than standing upright, a most unusual feature. Sadly, after having survived for perhaps 3000 years, the circle was vandalised by soldiers in 1940. Today only about half the stones remain, though the site is still very evocative.

(5) *Trawsfynydd Power Station*

The station sits at the side of the natural, but man-extended, Llyn Trawsfynydd. It is nuclear-powered, one of Britain's first generation Magnox stations, fuelled with natural uranium and generating 400 megawatts. Because it was constructed within the National Park, the station was designed, by Sir Basil Spence, to blend in with the surroundings, and landscaped by Dame Sylvia Crowe. The success of their ventures, both singly and jointly, is a matter of personal taste and opinion.

Walk 29 The Roman Steps to Rhinog Fawr

Half-way down the Rhinog ridge the ice sheets of the last Ice Age imposed their will on the hard Rhinog rock, carving two fine cwms. Cwm Nantcol we visit on Walk 30; here we go to Cwm Bychan, reached from Llanbedr on the coast road, the A496 Barmouth-Harlech road. At a bridge about 2 km (1¼ miles) from Llanbedr, Nantcol is over the bridge, while Bychan is straight on. Near the bridge, and signed from it, is Salem chapel, now famous (or should that be infamous?) for Curnow Vosper's picture of *The Welsh at prayer*. Vosper completed his picture in 1910, painting it

Llyn Trawsfynydd and the Arenigs from the Road's final col

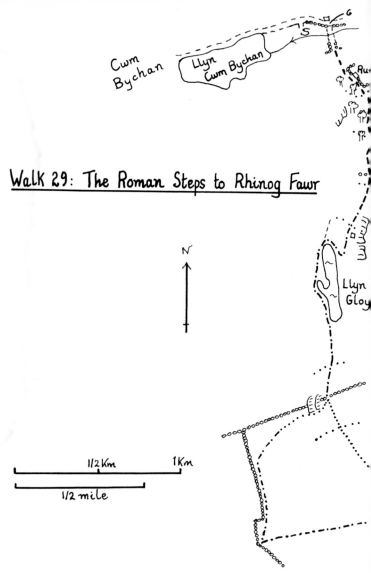

Cwm Bychan

Llyn Cwm Bychan

G

S

Ru

Llyn Gloy

Walk 29: The Roman Steps to Rhinog Fawr

N

1/2 Km   1 Km

1/2 mile

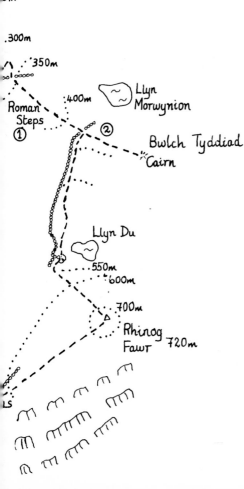

0m

.300m

.350m

Roman
Steps
① 400m

Llyn
Morwynion

② Bwlch Tyddiad
Cairn

Llyn Du

550m
600m

700m

Rhinog
Fawr   720m

LS

'live', the local people being paid sixpence for a sitting. Shani Owen stood as the central figure, a pious, but seemingly sour, old woman. The picture is famous for the Devil's head that many see in the folds of her shawl, though it has never been established whether this arose by accident or was a deliberate device by Vosper to accentuate what he saw as the hypocrisy of some of the church-goers.

Cwm Bychan is an idyllic valley from the outset, as the road winds narrowly through fine woodlands, but the lake near its head, Llyn Cwm Bychan, is the most picturesque spot of all. Hemmed in on its long sides by rough, tumbling crags, its upper end with a backdrop of the high Rhinog ridge, the whole surrounded by ancient oakwoods, it could easily still be the haunt of Celts or Arthurian knights.

The walk described is no simple route, all of the Rhinog walks being prone to difficult ground, but the Roman Steps are a worthy objective even if Rhinog Fawr is not your aim, and Cwm Bychan is certainly worth a trip.

Walk category: (a) Easy (1½ hours) via Roman Steps to Bwlch Tyddiad; (b) Intermediate (2½ hours) to Rhinog Fawr, returning by the same route; (c) Difficult (3 hours) complete route.

Length: (a) 5 km (3 miles); (b) 7 km (4½ miles); (c) 9 km (5¾ miles).

Ascent: (a) 275 m (900 ft); (b) 560 m (1850 ft); (c) 600 m (1970 ft).

Maps: Landranger Sheet 124; Outdoor Leisure Sheet 19.

Starting and finishing point: The car-park, at 645 315, at the head of Cwm Bychan, the cwm being reached as described in the introduction above.

The Roman Steps to Rhinog Fawr

Go right from the car-park to a signed path, right, through a gate.
The path crosses a stream and continues obviously through a small
broad-leaved wood to a gap in a wall. Beyond are the Roman Steps
(see (1) The Roman Steps) which are followed to another gap in a
wall and a notice announcing your entry into the Rhinog Nature
Reserve (see (2) Rhinog Nature Reserve). Ahead now is a large
cairn that marks the head of Bwlch Tyddiad, the crossing point of
this central section of the Rhinogs that the Roman Steps route used.
From the cairn there is a very fine view across the northern section
of the range. The lake to the left (north) is Llyn Morwynion,
another Lake of the Maidens (see the introduction to this, Rhinogs,
section). Return to the gap in the wall. (Return from here for the
Easy walk.)

Assuming now that you had just arrived at this gap from Cwm
Bychan, go through it and go right (south) along the wall, i.e. the
wall is at your right hand. Soon you pass another fine small lake,
Llyn Du, the Black Lake. Ahead now, the wall on your right is
attached to a crag, left, by a short wall section. Go over this and
continue for about 100 m, to where the path leaves the wall,
bending to the left away from it. Follow the path, which becomes a
little indistinct where scree lies, as it rises steeply to the summit of
Rhinog Fawr. (Return by the same route for the Intermediate
walk.)

From the summit, descend south-west down an obvious broad,
but tapering, ridge on a path heading for the wall ahead, meeting it
at a large cairn and another nature reserve notice. From here life
becomes difficult. The path leads on for about 800 m to a wall and,
turning right along the wall, i.e. with it at your left hand, and
following it around three right-angled bends, leads to a gap in it,
above Gloyw Llyn, after about 1200 m. Alternatively this gap can
be reached directly from our position by descending over very
rough country on a bearing of 332°. The gap is slightly east, 100 m or
so, of a prominent crag that the wall joins, but does not climb,
instead utilising it for a few metres. From the gap, however it is
reached, go down to the northern tip of Gloyw Llyn. An indistinct

Llyn Cwm Bychan

path follows the left shore line of the lake, rounding its northern tip.

At the tip a distinct path descends to Cwm Bychan and it is possible to follow this, but it is *not* a right of way.

After rounding the lake's tip, go back along the shore, heading south i.e. the wrong way!, for about 100 m to reach a path going left and up. Take this path, which leads down to rejoin the outward path just as the small deciduous wood is reached.

(1) *The Roman Steps*

It is probable that a route over Bwlch Tyddiad existed many years prior to the Roman occupation of Gwynedd. It is equally likely that it existed for many years after, so the name Roman is as good as any to apply to the route, an arithmetic mean of true ages!

What we now see, almost certainly, are the wide paving slabs of a medieval pack-horse trail, the steps needing to be very long so that horses could occasionally rest with all four hoofs at the same level. Later, the steps were also used as a drove road (see note (2) of Walk 31). The steps are, therefore, another link with history among the crags of this most ancient of landscapes. It is an interesting point to ponder from the glorious viewpoint of Bwlch Tyddiad, that the same view has excited or frustrated our ancestors for centuries.

(2) *Rhinog Nature Reserve*

The sheer poverty of the lands along the Rhinog ridge has meant that even sheep have been reluctant grazers, so that the original heather landscape, now eaten away on the other ranges we have crossed, is here still intact. The sheltering rock outcrops, and there are a great many, protect lichen in abundance, in addition to some interesting plant species, even a few orchids; ferns include the magnificent royal fern and the rare Tunbridge filmy-fern; and the bogs harbour several rarities.

At the head of Cwm Bychan you may see feral goats, though you will be very lucky to see any other mammals. The heather protects a few red grouse, while in the uplands you may see ring ouzels.

Walk 30   Rhinog Fach and Y Llethr

This route visits the other fine cwm mentioned in the introduction to
Walk 29, Cwm Nantcol. The two valleys could not be more
different: while Bychan is enclosed, Nantcol is open and airy,
offering a fine drive with excellent views. The walk itself climbs the
lower of the two Rhinog peaks, Rhinog Fach, and traverses one of
the most distinctive ridges in the whole area, that between Rhinog
Fach and Y Llethr.

Walk category: Difficult (4 hours).

Length: 12 km (7½ miles).

Ascent: 800 m (2620 ft).

Maps: Landranger Sheet 124; Outdoor Leisure Sheet 19.

Starting and finishing point: Near to Maes-y-garnedd at 642 269, at
the end of the Cwm Nantcol road. Parking places are very limited
and to maintain good relations with the local farmers it is imperative
that walkers park tidily and in a way that blocks no access or
thoroughfare.

From Maes-y-garnedd (see (1) Maes-y-garnedd) a signed path is
followed eastward, towards the obvious cleft of Bwlch Drws
Ardudwy. Occasionally the path is waymarked with white posts, but
is always obvious, passing, at one point, a notice announcing the
start of the Rhinog Nature Reserve (see note (2) of Walk 29) and
continuing right into the cleft and on to the Bwlch, the pass, itself
(see (2) The Rhinogs and Bwlch Drws Ardudwy). Beyond the
Bwlch, as the path starts to descend, an indistinct path right (south)
crosses a wall and continues to the top of Rhinog Fach, which,
typically in view of the number of walls in Cwm Nantcol (see (3)
Stone walls), is at the end of a wall. The more accepted ascent route
is reached by returning from the Bwlch to the end of the wall from
Maes-y-garnedd where another indistinct path gashes the summit.

Walk 30 : Rhinog Fach and Y Llethr

Bwlch Drus Ardudwy ②

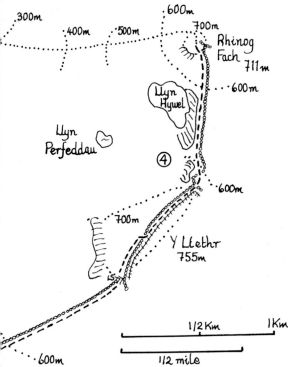

300m

400m   500m   600m

700m

Rhinog
Fach
711m

600m

Llyn
Hywel

600m

Llyn
Perfeddau

④

600m

700m

Y Llethr
755m

1/2 Km   1 Km

1/2 mile

600m

From the summit, follow another wall south, with the wall at your left hand, down to the pass between Rhinog Fach and Y Llethr, and on to the summit of the latter peak (reached by going through a gap in the wall!). At any convenient point, pause to view Llyn Hywel, the lake below the pass you have just crossed (see (4) Llyn Hywel and Y Llethr).

From the summit of Y Llethr continue along the wall to a junction of walls. Here a ladder stile is used to reach the far side of the wall going right (south of west). Follow this wall, i.e. have it at your right hand, until it turns sharply to the right. Now, 700 m away, almost due west and about 200 m below, another wall or, rather, the elbow of two walls can be seen. Go to the elbow and along the westward wall edge, i.e. have the wall at your right hand, for 80 m to a gate and ladder stile. Go over or through and take the distinct path beyond. The path traverses two old walls and, near a stream, uses a gate to cross a third. Beyond, the path leads easily to the Cwm Nantcol road. Go right, and follow the unfenced road beyond to Maes-y-garnedd.

(1) *Maes-y-garnedd*

The farm was the birthplace and early home of John Jones, who left Cwm Nantcol to be an apprentice in London. When the Civil War started Jones joined the Parliamentarians, rising to the rank of colonel, and marrying Oliver Cromwell's sister, Catherine. He became an MP and was one of the signatories of Charles II's death warrant. After the restoration Colonel Jones was tried as a regicide, found guilty and sentenced to a traitor's death. Samuel Pepys notes in his diary that one day as he was out walking the 'steaming remains' of Jones were towed by, after he had been hung, drawn and quartered.

(2) *The Rhinogs and Bwlch Drws Ardudwy*

The Bwlch is the Pass of the Door of Ardudwy, *rhinog* meaning doorpost, the two Rhinog peaks standing to each side of the Bwlch. The pass is another old drover's road (see note (2) of Walk 31).

Rhinog Fach and the Y Llethr slabs

(3) *Stone walls*

Of all the areas we shall visit, Cwm Nantcol is the most astonishing for dry-stone walls. Not just for their abundance, although the labour involved in the construction of such walls is amazing – a good waller could manage about a chain per day (a unit that not only translates poorly into metric units, a chain being 20.1168 metres, but is not even happy with a translation into imperial units) but for the ingenuity, the sheer civil engineering brilliance, with which rock outcrops were utilised and steep slopes overcome, raising the standard of wall-building to an art form.

(4) *Llyn Hywel and Y Llethr*

Llyn Hywel lies in an ice-carved hollow, the ice-chamfered slabs of Y Llethr rising steeply from it. The combination of lake and slabs, with a backdrop of rugged Rhinog Fach, is one of the most memorable views in Snowdonia. The small lake to the south-west of Llyn Hywel is Llyn Perfeddau, the name translating not as Perfect Lake, as a first glance might suggest, but as Lake of Entrails!

Walk 31   The Drovers' Road

This walk follows an old road across the moorland in the south of the Rhinog range, but starts near the coast, visiting two of the fine neolithic sites of the area.

Walk category: Intermediate (3¾ hours).

Length: 14.5 km (9 miles).

Ascent: 350 m (1150 ft).

Maps: Landranger Sheet 124; Outdoor Leisure Sheet 19.

Starting and finishing point: Dyffryn Ardudwy, on the A496 Barmouth-Harlech road, about 5 miles north of Barmouth.

The Drovers' Road

Walk 31 : The Drovers' Road

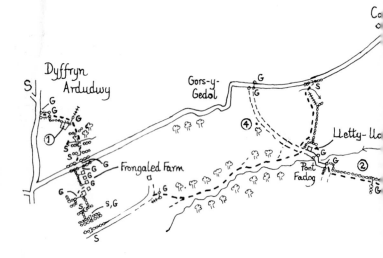

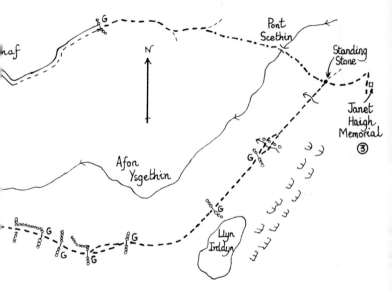

haf

G

N

Pont
Scethin

Standing
Stone

Janet
Haigh
Memorial

③

Afon
Ysgethin

G

G

G

G

G

G

Llyn
Irddyn

From the main road take the lane beside the school to the first
burial chamber (see (1) Dyffryn Burial Chamber). Continue on the
same lane, past woodland, to a minor road. Go across and follow a
marked path across fields and, at one point, an astonishingly wide
wall crossed by what could be termed a parapet rather than a stile,
to a metalled lane. Go left and follow to where it bends left to a
farm. Here go ahead into woodland. At the first Y-junction go
right, at the second go right again. This path meets another at a
stream. Follow this, going ahead to stay close to the stream where
the broader path goes off left, to a small cottage called Lletty-lloegr.
Go left on the road, and right almost immediately on a path going
around behind the cottage, to follow a wall away from the cottage.
Where the wall meets a fence, follow the fence, go over a stream
and use a stile to reach a lane. Go right.

The lane continues between walls for about 2 km (1¼ miles), and
where it ends a track heads off across the moor. About 500 m from
the end of the wall a path goes off right. Ignore this, but where
another path goes off right, near a cairn after another 200 m, we
take that path to Pont Scethin (see (2) The Drovers' Road).

Beyond the bridge an indistinct path crosses boggy ground to
reach a standing stone. Go straight on taking the narrow path that
climbs towards Diffwys, the highest peak of the Rhinogs, as far as
the memorial stone (see (3) Janet Haigh Memorial). Return to the
standing stone. Now go left (south-west). Those who have decided
not to visit the memorial stone go right when they reach the
standing stone from Pont Scethin. The track crosses fine moorland,
going close to Llyn Irddyn, nestling below the crags of Llawlech.
When another track crosses, at a T-junction, go right to a gate.
Beyond is a metalled road to Pont Fadog, and on to Lletty-lloegr.

Do not retrace the outward route, but go on along the road to
reach another burial chamber (see (4) Gors-y-Gedol Burial
Chamber). At the road end a gate leads to another road. Go left to
return to Dyffryn.

Mist shrouded Pont Scethin

(1) *Dyffryn Burial Chamber*

These interesting chambers were thoroughly excavated in 1962, the excavations revealing some pieces of late neolithic pottery and a collection of cremated bones.

(2) *The Drovers' Road*

The cottage name Lletty-lloegr means English Shelter, for this was an overnight stop and emergency shoeing station for drovers on the road to England. The drovers were the medieval equivalent of cowboys, herding animals to markets far from where they were raised when, before refrigeration, meat had to be delivered on the hoof. A large drove must have been a wonderful sight because good drovers took not only cows and sheep, but pigs, geese and turkeys. All the animals were prepared for the drove, the emergency shoeing station probably being to replace the shoes of bulls. It was said that the smiths who shod bulls were both skilled and brave and I can certainly believe the latter! The poultry were prepared for the drove by having their feet encased in pitch.

Pont Scethin, now a surprising sight, a bridge in the middle of nowhere, took the droves over the Afon Ysgethin, as indeed did Pont Fadog for those who crossed further west. Later Pont Scethin took the London mail coach from Harlech, the coach then toiling up the slopes of Diffwys beyond. A fully laden coach, with four in hand, must have been as grand a sight as a full drove.

(3) *Janet Haigh Memorial*

This fine memorial is for a mother by a son. Dr Melvyn Haigh, Bishop of Winchester, erected the slate in memory of his mother Janet who died in 1953. The stone relates that 'even as late as her eighty-fourth year, despite dim sight and stiffened joints' she 'still loved to walk this way'. The inscription ends with the simple, but dignified, 'Courage Traveller.' What a great pity that some idiot has vandalised the slab.

On a clear day you can see Snowdon from this spot.

(4) *Gors-y-Gedol Burial Chamber*

Sometimes called Arthur's Quoit, this chamber has been much damaged since its construction. Once it was the chamber in a wedge-shaped mound 25 m (82 ft) long and 10 m (33 ft) wide. The huge capstone measure 3.5×3 m ($11\frac{1}{2} \times 10$ ft) and weighs many tons. The chamber shares features with others, not only in Snowdonia, but in Northern Ireland and south-west Scotland.

Walk 32   Coed-y-Brenin Forest

To the south-east of our area, as the Rhinogs fall away to the valley of the Afon Mawddach and the Cambrian sub-strata give way to Ordovician sub-strata, is the Coed-y-Brenin Forest.

Coed-y-Brenin is the King's Forest, a name that does not derive from any king of an old Welsh kingdom, though Cadwgan, Prince of Powys, did have a hunting estate here, but commemorates the Silver Jubilee of George V in 1935.

Our route explores the forest, visiting one of the famous Dolgellau gold mines and several excellent waterfalls, and making full use of location markers within the forest which – together with a map of the forest available from the Maesgwm Forest Centre, at 715 276, reached by going left off the A470 north of Ganllwyd – should ensure that the forest visitor does not stay lost for long. However, not all of the location markers are always in position, and the map has some ambiguities, so please be careful.

Walk category: Easy/Intermediate (2¾ hours).

Length: 11.5 km (7¼ miles).

Ascent: 200 m (650 ft).

Maps: Landranger Sheet 124; Outdoor Leisure Sheets 18 and 23; Forestry Commission map (see introduction above).

Starting and finishing point: The car-park at 727 245 beside the A470 in Ganllwyd – to the right if travelling north – or the Forestry Commission car-park, again a so-called car-park, being neither large nor surfaced, nor even very clearly defined, at Location Post 27 (at 732 251), reached by going right off the A470 just beyond Ganllwyd.

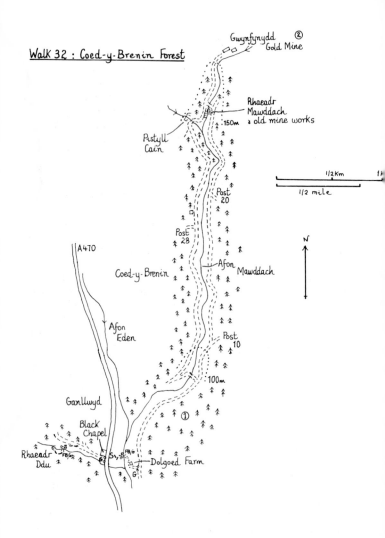

Walk 32 : Coed-y-Brenin Forest

Gwynfynydd ②
Gold Mine

Rhaeadr
Mawddach
& old mine works

150m

Pistyll
Cain

Post
20

Post
28

A470

Coed-y-Brenin

Afon
Mawddach

Afon
Eden

Post
10

100m

Ganllwyd

Black
Chapel

①

Rhaeadr
Ddu

Dolgoed Farm

½ Km   1 K

½ mile

N

From the car-park go down the path to the picnic site and a bridge, over the Afon Mawddach. Go over the bridge and right, across the field to the farmhouse. Go round this to its right, actually going along the house path and up the drive to a gate. Beyond is a forest road (see (1) Coed-y-Brenin). Go left. Follow the road to Location Post 10, at a Y-junction. Take the left branch and continue past Post 20 to Post 19. As Post 19 is approached, Rhaeadr Mawddach will be heard, the falls being surprisingly loud for their size.

After crossing the Afon Mawddach go right to the Gwynfynydd Gold Mine (see (2) Gold mining), retracing the route to the bridge after the visit. Now, do not cross the bridge but go ahead following the path to cross the Afon Gain. From the bridge there is an excellent view of our second waterfall, Pistyll Cain.

Beyond the bridge the path reaches Post 29, where the forestry map shows a road that is not present. Follow the forest road that is a continuation of the road over the bridge, passing Ferndale to Post 28 and on to Post 27 and the forestry car-park. Here, cross the bridge (not clearly marked on the forestry map) to rejoin the outward road. Go right, retracing the outward walk to the car-park.

Having got this close it would be a shame to miss Rhaeadr Ddu, the most impressive of the three waterfalls. It has been called eerie and sinister, its waters having been said to slide down a black chute into a black pit, but it is also a fine waterfall, well set among oak and beech woods. It is reached by crossing the A470 from the car park and going through a gate beside the black, corrugated chapel. Follow the road for about 400 m to an obvious path left that leads over a footbridge to a good viewpoint.

(1) *Coed-y-Brenin*

The forest covers over 6300 hectares (15 500 acres – nearly 25 sq miles) and is chiefly coniferous. As is usual sitka spruce and Norwegian spruce are the predominant species, though there is quite a variety, including Noble and Douglas fir and the native Scots pine. There are few areas of broadleaf, but some, oak and beech in the main, have been planted. Annual timber production exceeds 25 000 cubic m (about 882 250 cubic ft). If you think of a plank 6 ft long, 6 ins wide and 1 in thick, the forest produces 3½ million of those every year.

Many of Britain's mammals are present in the forest, including the elusive fallow deer and polecat, and the rare and elusive pine marten. Bird life is more limited, the dense conifer stands not being a particularly good habitat, but several members of the crow family are in residence, as is the green woodpecker, while on higher ground there are black grouse, though not many.

(2) *Gold mining*

Although the Romans are known to have mined gold in old Carmarthenshire, there is no evidence that they ever worked it in what is now the Coed-y-Brenin. The first confirmed discovery was as late as 1843, when a find in an old lead mine started a minor gold rush with two dozen mines and over a hundred shafts opening within ten years.

The Gwynfynydd mine that we visit was the richest of all the Dolgellau mines, producing as much as 18 oz of gold from a ton of ore, and is still in operation. Visitors are not allowed on to the site, but a board explains the history of gold mining in the area.

Rhaeadr Mawddach was used to power the Gwynfynydd operation, and the ruins near the falls are the remains of a processing plant. Here the ore was crushed by a heavy stone 'breaker', then stamped to a fine powder by an iron stamp weighing around a ton: there were 40 stamps here when Gwynfynydd was at its height. The powder was then water-borne over mercury-coated plates, the gold-mercury amalgam formed being processed to produce pure gold.

DOLGELLAU

Near Dolgellau are two very fine short walks that can be completed as a pair, giving a superb mix of scenery.

Rhaeadr Ddu

Walk 33 a) Torrent Walk

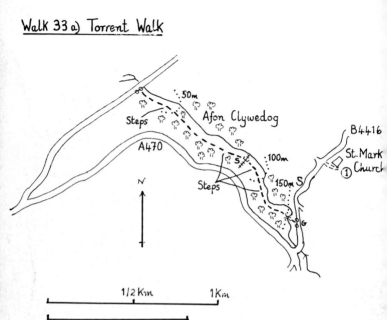

Walk 33 The Torrent Walk and the Precipice Walk

Walk category: (a) Torrent Walk, Easy (¾ hour). (b) Precipice Walk, Easy (1½ hours).

Length: (a) Torrent Walk, 2.5 km (1½ miles). (b) Precipice Walk, 6 km (3¾ miles).

Ascent: (a) Torrent Walk, 115 m (375 ft). (b) Precipice Walk, 50 m (165 ft).

Maps: Landranger Sheet 124; Outdoor Leisure Sheet 23.

The Torrent Walk

(a) The Torrent Walk

The Torrent Walk was laid out by Thomas Payne, a surveyor and engineer, during a ten-year period from 1799, assisted by his son (also Thomas). Payne also designed and engineered the famous cob at Porthmadog. In its original form, the walk's return route was on the river's right bank, but this path has long since reverted to farmland. The walk is breathtakingly beautiful at most times of the year, the fine rush and tumble of the river being complemented by spring flowers, summer leaves, autumn's colours or winter's bareness.

Starting and finishing point: Lay-bys near the signed start of the walk at 761 181 on the B4416, Brithdir road, off the A470, about 4 km (2½ miles) from Dolgellau towards Machynlleth. There is space for only one or two cars at the top of the walk, but a few metres further along there is a larger lay-by.

From the road the signed path leads to a footbridge, beyond which a path, with sections of steps, leads down the left bank of the Afon Clywedog to a minor road. Return up the path, a return route nowhere near as dull as it seems, as there is always something new to see. From the top of the walk it is worth going along the B4416 to visit St Mark's church (see (1) St Mark's church).

(1) St Mark's church

This fine church was built as late as 1895, and its churchyard holds the remains of Constance Farrar, aunt of Montgomery of Alamein, and of the Misses Brown, aunts of Admiral Lord Cunningham. It is its interior, however, which holds the most interesting items, beaten copper panels by the art nouveau artist Henry Wilson. The panels, to the altar, reredos and pulpit, are remarkable, and come as quite a surprise. More traditionally beautiful are the choir stalls of Spanish chestnut.

Walk 33 b) Precipice Walk

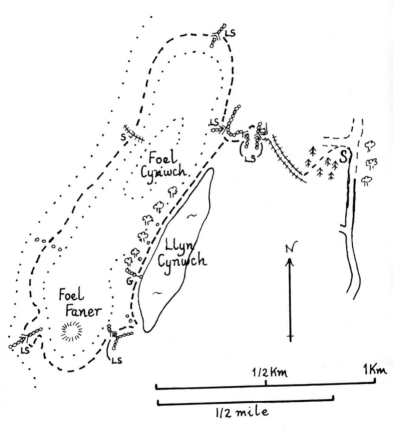

(b) The Precipice Walk

It is believed that sheep contouring around the twin peaks of
Foel Cynwch and Foel Faner started the Precipice Walk, though
it is now tended by the National Park Authority. The walk is *not*
a public right of way, but a permissive path on the Nannau
estate, so it is imperative that walkers obey all signs and consider
at all times that it is on their actions that the next walkers will be
judged.

The precipice of the name is on the western section of the
walk, and while it will be of little concern to anyone with
mountain-walking experience it has given the odd nasty turn to
the inexperienced. Nowhere is the walk dangerous, however, and
it does offer excellent views to Snowdon, the Moelwyns, the
Rhinogs, Arans and Arenigs, over Coed-y-Brenin and most
especially to Cadair Idris towering over Dolgellau and the
Mawddach estuary.

Starting and finishing point: Car-park at 746 212 to the left of the
road to Llanfachreth reached from the A494 Dolgellau–Bala
road.

From the car-park go left on a minor road that leaves the
Llanfachreth road near the car-park, and after a few metres go
left through a gate on a signed path to a cottage. Just before the
cottage go left over a ladder stile and shortly go over another to
reach a Y-junction of paths. The arms of the Y are the outward
and return paths of the walk. It is usual to go anticlockwise, i.e.
to take the path to the right. There are several stiles on the
circuit, the western arm of which has most of the views. The
return leg is beside the delightful Llyn Cynwch.

Foel Faner, around which the Precipice Walk winds, from the Afon Mawddach

CADAIR IDRIS

As we completed the Precipice Walk (Walk 33b), what took the eye was the huge northern wall of Cadair Idris towering above the Mawddach estuary. Pen-y-gadair, the high point of Cadair Idris, is not the highest mountain in the southern half of the Snowdonia National Park, that honour falling to Aran Mawddwy by all of 13 m (43 ft). But it is to Cadair that the tourists flock, not to the Arans, and this migration has little to do with the relative inaccessibility of the latter range. It is because Cadair Idris has presence.

The volcanic igneous rock – here a very hard granite-like rock called granophyre which is not common in the Park – combined with the effects of glaciation have sculpted a magnificent terrain, a series of back-to-back cwms, the ridges that divide them carved to knife-edges in places, the back walls of the cwms sliced steep and high. Cwm Cadair is the most famous of the cwms, north-facing and protected by the long arête of Cyfrwy, its over-deepened basin filled by Llyn y Gadair. The back wall, the northern wall of Pen-y-gadair itself, is diagonally banded, a structure that is delightfully picked out by a low-lying sun. To the south the back wall of Cwm Cau is even steeper, the tall cliffs offering high-quality rock climbing. Cwm Cau is tighter, its own lake, Llyn Cau, touched by steep cliffs on three sides, the fourth protected by a ridge of moraine. If Cwm Cadair is the more famous, Cwm Cau is the more beautiful.

To the east of the high peaks, the shattered nature of the terrain shifts from the northern face to the southern, a long row of crags and steep gullies overlooking the main A487 road. To the west Cadair falls away to some fine scenery, which includes Craig yr Aderyn, Bird Rock.

One oddity in the glaciated landscape is Llyn Mwyngil, the Tal-y-llyn Lake, which is not glacial at all, but has formed behind an ancient landslide.

Tal-y-llyn Lake from Walk 34

Walk 34   Cwm Cau and Cadair Idris

The Minffordd Path, which we follow at first, starts very low and so involves a lot of climbing to reach the highest point of Cadair Idris. In exchange for this, it passes through some varied and delightful scenery and in Cwm Cau – as mentioned above – the finest of the Snowdonian cwms, which from the right vantage point at its entrance seems to be perfection in mountain architecture.

Walk category: Difficult (3¾ hours).

Length: 10 km (6¼ miles).

Ascent: 1000 m (3280 ft).

Maps: Landranger Sheet 124; Outdoor Leisure Sheet 23.

Starting and finishing point: At 730 114, at the very start of the walk near the wrought-iron gates of the old Idris estate, there is space for three or four cars. Thankfully this spot, traditionally the only spot and requiring an early start or crossed fingers, is now supplemented by a larger car park a few metres north-east i.e. towards the Cross Foxes, away from Tal-y-llyn.

From the gate beside the fine old estate gates go up an old drive, with excellent rhododendron bushes and an avenue of grand Scots pine. A stream now runs among the pines, and in wet weather the avenue can be damp. At the drive's end a gate gives access to the nature reserve (see (1) Cadair Idris Nature Reserve). Within the reserve the walker must keep to the path which winds steeply up through fine woodland, with excellent views to the tumbling stream of Nant Cadair.

At a gate the wood is left behind. The path is still distinct and rising steadily, at one point doubling back to avoid an obvious boggy patch, and swinging around left so that Cwm Cau is opened

Llyn Cau from Craig Cau

Walk 34 : Cwm Cau and Cadair Idris

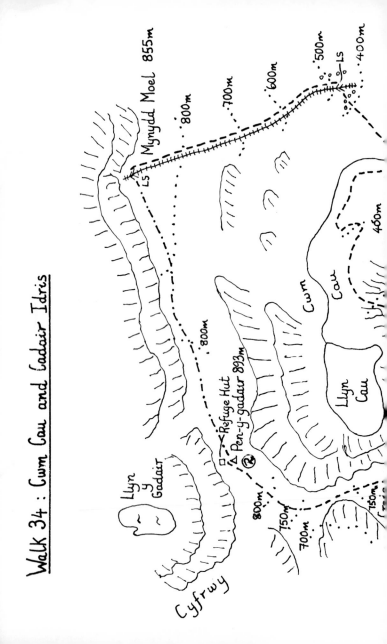

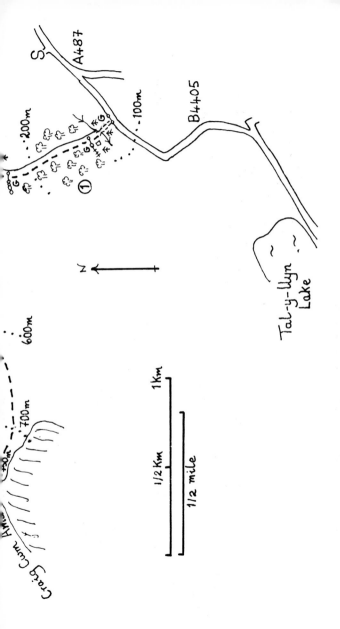

up. At a large cairn the left-hand of two paths is followed, but the right-hand path should be taken, if only briefly, as the best view, at this level, of Cwm Cau is towards the far side of the lake where the stream leaves it.

The left-hand path rises steeply up the ridge of Craig Cau, with tremendous views across the cwm, reaching the summit. From here the view south-west, of Mynydd Pencoed and the parallel valleys of Tal-y-llyn and of the Afon Dysynni, is superb.

Ahead, the ridge drops to Bwlch Cau before rising on a rightward curve to the summit of Pen-y-gadair. In the early stages of this climb from Bwlch Cau take care not to wander too close to the top of Craig Cau. It is unforgivingly steep. The summit of Pen-y-gadair has an Ordnance Survey triangulation pillar and, most unusually, a refuge (but see (2) Cadair Idris).

From Pen-y-gadair go north-east, ignoring the path that descends into Cwm Cadair, but admiring the view, over rocky ground to a more gentle plateau that offers good views across the northern face. Continue to the obvious rounded summit of Mynydd Moel.

From Mynydd Moel go south-east, to follow the wall down. The right (west) side of this ridge offers excellent views into Cwm Cau, but do not go too far west as the ground becomes broken with rock outcrops. When a ladder stile is reached use it to gain a path that goes diagonally across the slope to meet the outward path at the top of the wooded section. Ford the stream and reverse the outward route.

(1) *Cadair Idris Nature Reserve*

A permit is required for the enclosed woodland of this reserve.
Several British alpine species have their southern limit here, and the occasional burst of lime-rich – well, perhaps not rich, but lime-y – rock accounts for the presence of some very good, though difficult to find, species (alpine and lesser meadow-rues, green spleenwort) together with more common plants (mountain sorrel and purple saxifrage) and some very rare finds (moss campion, dwarf willow and stiff sedge). The broad-leaved woodland beside the stream is a

Cyfrwy from Pen y gadair

rich site for flora, but this must be viewed from the paths if you have no permit.

(2) *Cadair Idris*

Cadair Idris means the Chair of Idris, the chair generally believed to refer specifically to Cwm Gadair, with the northern cliffs as back and the Cyfrwy arête as a fine left armrest. On Idris, opinions are more divided. He is said to have been a giant, one of the many, but that is too vague, and the only giant genuinely connected with the peak is Gwyn ap Nudd who hunted the hills with a dog pack searching for the souls of those killed on the cliffs. Others contend that he was a prince, Idris ap Gwyddno, who is known to have fought a battle against the Saxons (or was it the Irish?), in 630, winning the battle but being killed in it. That battle is referred to as the Slaughter of the Severn, which is over on Plynlimon, a bit too far away from the peak for an obvious connection. Lastly, Idris is said to have been a Celtic poet who sat on the peak and mused. This sounds like a way of tying in the famous saying that anyone who spends a night alone on Pen-y-gadair will be, by morning, a poet or a madman. But that saying was first attached to Clogwyn d'ur Arddu, near Snowdon, and has only recently been transferred to Cadair Idris.

The suggestions are romantic, and there has always been a great deal of romance attached to Cadair. In the last century tourists flocked to it, to be guided to the top. The new refuge on the top replaces a much more amateur one in which an old lady – a very, very old lady if the tales are true – sold tea to the tourists! Charles Darwin came this way noting that 'Old Cadair is a grand fellow and shows himself off superbly with ever changing light'. A bit flippant perhaps, but also a strange echo of an *englyn* – a particular form of Welsh verse – by the bard Gwilym Cowlyd:

> The calm green lakes are sleeping in the mountain shadow
> And on the water's canvas bright sunshine paints the picture of
> the day.

Gwilym wrote this, in Welsh of course, about Cadair Idris.

Walk 35   Castell-y-Bere

To the south-west of high Pen-y-gadair, Cadair Idris forms a long, peaked ridge between the Tal-y-llyn and Dysynni valleys. On the flank of one peak is the Welsh castle of Castell-y-Bere. This walk visits that site and crosses the ridge between the two valleys.

Walk category: Easy/Intermediate (2½ hours).

Length: 10 km (6¾ miles).

Ascent: 150 m (500 ft).

Maps: Landranger Sheet 124; Outdoor Leisure Sheet 23.

Starting and finishing point: Several are possible on this circular walk: the car-park at Castell-y-Bere (688 086), though this should not be used if there is a large number of visitors, Llanfihangel-y-Pennant, reached by road from Abergynolwyn in the Tal-y-llyn valley, or Abergynolwyn itself.

As the footpath from the car park to Castell-y-Bere (see (1) Castel-y-Bere) doubles back on itself to the right, down left among the trees is an unsigned ladder stile. Go over this and down through the small wood to a stream. Ford the stream, cross the fence and go right along it, i.e. have it at your right hand. Where there are old and new barns go through a gate, right, to a road. A short version of the walk goes down this road to Llanfihangel-y-Pennant. Go left and follow the road to the farm. A gate in the far left corner of the farmyard leads to a muddy path and footbridge. Go over the bridge, turn right and follow the straightforward path to Mary Jones' Cottage (see (2) Mary Jones).

   From the cottage go south down the road to the church (see (3) Llanfihangel-y-Pennant). There turn left opposite the church to a car park, where a signed path beside the stream leads past a house into a beautiful section of oak woodland. The path through this is obvious, with occasional yellow arrows on trees, going up away

Walk 35 : Castell-y-Bere

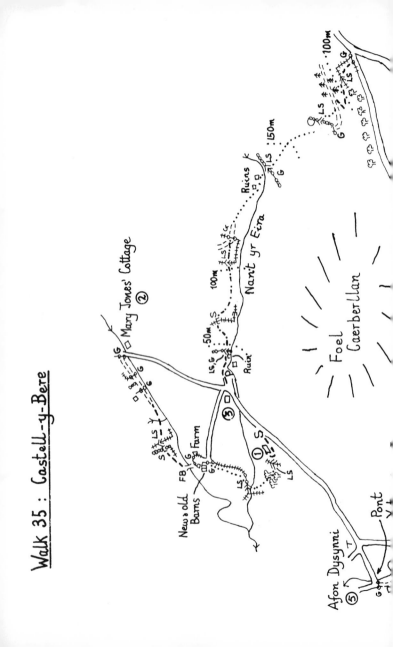

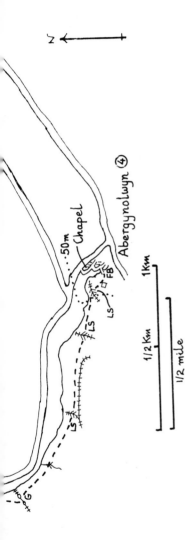

N ←——→

....50m

Chapel

FB

Abergynolwyn ④

LS

LS

LS

G

1Km   1/2 Km

1/2 mile

from the stream at one point to reach a stile. When a track is reached, go right along it, through a gate to more open country.

Head now for the ruined farmhouse ahead, a ladder stile beyond which gives access to more open, pathless ground. Go ahead, then up and right to sheep pens. A ladder stile here gives access to a distinct track. Follow this around a left-hand bend to woodland. There watch for a yellow-topped post that marks the start of a woodland path going down and right. Follow this, there are more yellow-topped posts, to a fence and ladder stile. Go over and down to a gate and the road. Go right, and left at a T-junction to Abergynolwyn (see (4) Abergynolwyn).

At the chapel to the right soon after the village is reached go right along a lane (Water Street) that goes behind the chapel, and first right to another lane. From this a footbridge goes off right. Take this and the distinct path beyond which rises and swings right past Gamallt farm, before taking a line parallel to the Afon Dysynni, to Rhiwlas farm. Go past the farm, with it on your left hand, and down its drive to the road. Go right (see (5) The Dysynni valley) over the Pont Ystumanner and on to a crossroads with a telephone box to the left. Go ahead to return to Castell-y-Bere.

(1) *Castell-y-Bere*

Castell-y-Bere was one of the greatest of the Welsh, as opposed to English, castles in Wales, its relative lack of niceties – there was no portcullis, for instance – being made up for by a strong natural position and formidable masonry. The castle was begun by Llywelyn the Great, probably as late as 1221, and was the seat of the Princes of Wales until Llywelyn the Last abandoned it to Edward I in 1282. Edward partially destroyed it, seeing it more as a symbol of Welsh independence than as a defensive castle, and though it was briefly retaken by the Welsh in 1294 it was too damaged to be credible, and was abandoned.

The ruin is a romantic one, dramatically set among scenery that exemplifies Wales, with Cadair Idris rising behind it. From it there is a fine view of Craig yr Aderyn, Bird Rock.

Craig yr Aderyn (Bird Rock) from Castell-y-Bere

(2) *Mary Jones*

The ruined cottage of Tyn-y-ddôl was once the home of Mary Jones, an ordinary Welsh girl who performed the far-from-ordinary feat, in 1800, of trekking – barefoot and alone, at the age of sixteen – to Bala, a round trip of 50 miles, to buy a Bible for which she had saved long and hard. When she arrived the minister, Thomas Charles, had sold his last Welsh Bible, but was so moved by the girl's action that he founded the British and Foreign Bible Society. The Society still holds the Bible it gave to Mary, whose trek is commemorated at the ruin of her house.

(3) *Llanfihangel-y-Pennant*

This village, little bigger it seems than its name, is beautifully sited, and has a fine church. The church has a lepers' window – in its north wall beside the vestry door – dating from the time when leprosy was rife in the area and lepers were only allowed to view services through the window. The fine font is of local stone, while the lectern holds an early Welsh Bible. The excellent lych-gate has slate slabs over a cattle grid installed to prevent animals entering the churchyard.

(4) *Abergynolwyn*

This town, now famous for its association with a 'great little train', the Talyllyn Railway, was built for workers in the Bryneglwys slate quarry to the south-east of the town. For its time it was very socially advanced, with a grid layout and many facilities not available to slate workers in the north. Today the townsfolk are mainly employed by the Forestry Commission, though a link with the past exists in the fine museum of the slate industry.

(5) *The Dysynni valley*

The Dysynni valley takes an odd right and left from here, transferring from the Tal-y-llyn valley, and the river's source, Talyllyn Lake, to a parallel valley. Geographically this is an 'elbow of river capture' where a blockage in a valley, most probably in this case a landslip in the Tal-y-llyn, causes a river to find another outlet to the sea.

Llanfihangel-y-Pennant church

THE ARANS

The Arans form a high, narrow ridge running north-south from the end of Bala Lake to the valleys around Dinas Mawddwy. These valleys, isolated from the outside world by high passes – none more so than Bwlch Oerddrws, the Pass of the Cold Door, aptly named when winter's winds blow, and Bwlch y Groes, the Pass of the Cross, the cross (no longer extant) having been erected by a thankful traveller at the spot where he had evaded a ghostly rider – were a kingdom until the early thirteenth century. Then Llywelyn the Great forced open the cold door and made the leaders of the valley kingdom pledge allegiance to him. Much later, during the reign of Queen Anne, the valleys were home to a group of red-haired bandits who terrorised the area beyond the passes, robbing and killing. One Christmas Eve a local baron gathered a large force and invaded the valleys, capturing 80 of the group, many of whom were condemned to death. The mother of two of the younger men pleaded with the baron for their young lives, but was refused. She cursed him, promising that her kin would wash their hands in his blood if the executions were carried out. They were, and soon after, at Llidiart-y-Barwn, the Baron's Gate, the baron and his son were stabbed to death. The murder led to further reprisals and today the band lives on only in the name of the inn at Mallwyd, the Brigands' Inn, and in the trademark of Mallwyd's Meirion Mill.

The Arans are not a magnetic range, for walkers or compasses, attracting few visitors despite Aran Mawddwy being higher than Cadair Idris's highest peak. There is some fine scenery, however, nowhere better than the beautifully named Craiglyn Dyfi, the lake that is the birthplace of the Dyfi, one of Wales's finest rivers, which nestles under the eastern cliff of Aran Mawddwy. Sadly, however, there have been access difficulties on the range with the position constantly changing: no access, access by single permissive pass and so on. At present there is limited access to the range, and though it is easy to extend the suggested walk to include a visit to the high tops, and even to produce a circular walk by returning down Cwm Hengwm, the straightforward out-and-back walk does make the best of the easily available scenery.

Walk 36 : Cwm Cowarch

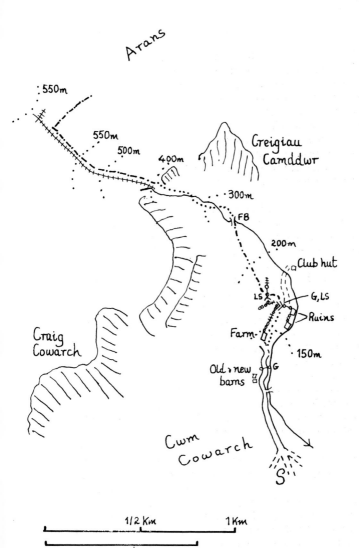

Walk 36   Cwm Cowarch

Cwm Cowarch is a magnificent cwm, indeed the archetypal cwm, with its flat-bottomed U-shape, high, parallel, enclosing ridges, and the cliffs of Craig Cowarch along the backwall. Our route takes the path from the Cwm towards Rhydymain, reaching the pass that the path uses to breach the wild and high Arans ridge. Though relatively short, the route is not well defined, and crosses some quite steep and rugged, though breathtaking, country.

Walk category: Intermediate (2¼ hours).

Length: 6½ km (4 miles).

Ascent: 500 m (1650 ft).

Maps: Landranger Sheet 124; Outdoor Leisure Sheet 23.

Starting and finishing point: There is no car park at the head of Cwm Cowarch, at 853 187, reached by minor road from Dinas Mawddwy on the A470, but the large area of common allows parking. Please be both tidy and considerate; this is a sensitive area.

Go along the valley road towards its end (it is sign-posted a 'No Through Road') passing a bridge that takes a second access path to Cwm Hengwm, and a pair of barns to the left. One is old and sadly dilapidated, a building of stone, slate and character. The other is modern and complete, a building of concrete block, corrugated metal and utterly characterless. Go through a gate to reach a signed green path that leaves the farm lane rightwards. The path is sometimes also a meandering stream that needs occasional fording. Ignore a bridge, right, to follow the path around the farm and then rightwards along a wall. The farmhouse wall here is inscribed in brick 'E.B. 1873' an inscription by someone who was not shy and retiring. Follow the path to a ladder stile beyond which are the spoil

Cwm Cowarch

heaps of old mines, and a shale road to the climbers' club hut. We go left, however, on a path signed to Rhydymain and the Arans that is nowhere distinct, but always obvious. The country here is magnificent, wild and rocky – though with the occasional, and quite surprising, tree – an increasingly narrow gorge with the crags of Craig Cowarch to the left and the steep scree slopes of Creigiau Camddwr to the right. On those slopes are some of the finest *roche moutonnée* in Wales. Beyond a landslip scar, go above or below this, the very indistinct path is marked by yellow arrows on rocks, a 'vandalism' that is necessary to mark the access path. A footbridge is used to cross the gorge's stream at one point, though a more personal arrangement must be made when it is crossed again. As the gorge narrows care is needed with the route which is steep and rocky. A fence is reached and followed to the pass with its small lake.

From the lake go right, north-east, to gain a good viewpoint of the high Arans ridge further to the north-east – the high Arans peaks are easily reached from here, Aran Fawddwy being about 2 km (1¼ miles) away and 300 m (1000 ft) higher – and of the fine peak to the south-west, one of Wales's most elusive 2500 ft peaks.

Return is back down the outward route.

Appendices

Offa's Dyke Path

The Offa's Dyke Path is the only official long-distance footpath to cross North Wales, and even that does not enter the Snowdonia National Park. The route starts (or ends) at Prestatyn, going south over the Clwydian Hills – Walk 6 follows part of the path over the Clwydians – to Llangollen, traversing mid-Wales to the Black Mountains which it follows into South Wales, to finish at Chepstow.

See *Offa's Dyke Path*, Christopher John Wright, a Constable Guide.

The Cambrian Way

Despite strenuous efforts by the Countryside Commission to find a pathway through the conflicting desires of walkers' interest groups, countryside interest groups and farmers, the attempt to produce a Cambrian Way was finally abandoned in 1982. The route was to have started in Cardiff and traversed all of the main Welsh mountain blocks – including Cadair Idris, the Rhinogs, the Moelwyns, Snowdon, the Glyders and the Carneddau – to finish at Conwy.

A guide to a personal interpretation of the projected route has been published by the author of this guide – see *A Cambrian Way*, Richard Sale, a Constable Guide.

The Welsh Three-Thousanders

Wales has fourteen peaks of more than 3000 ft, three on Snowdon, five on the Glyders and six on the Carneddau, and the climbing of these in one continuous walk within 24 hours is a well-known test piece. There seems to be no set route for the completion of the journey. The author favours an east-west traverse because it climbs Tryfan's north ridge, Bristly Ridge and Crib Goch, rather than descending them, though walkers of merit have spoken in favour of a west-east traverse. Either way the route is obvious enough, the outliers of Yr Elen (on the Carneddau) and Elidir Fawr (on the

Glyders) offering scope for frustration.

The peaks have been raced over and, for all I know, traversed on unicycles. Ignore the hype of all previous journeys and journeyers: come in a spirit of communion not competition. There are fourteen peaks of note in both Wales and the Himalayas, and if the Himalayan peaks are famed for being more than 8000 m high, each topping its Welsh counterpart eight-fold in height, the difference is only a matter of degree. As Maurice Herzog noted after the ascent, and epic descent, of Annapurna, the first of the 8000 m peaks to be climbed: 'There are other Annapurnas in the lives of men.'

Other shorter walks and trails

The Nature Conservancy Council publishes leaflets on nature trails in Coedydd Aber, Cwm y Llan, Cwm Idwal and Coed Llyn Mair.

The National Park Committee publishes leaflets on walks around Maentwrog; the Snowdon Range, Llanberis, Rhyd Ddu, Watkin and Miners' Paths to Snowdon; the Minffordd, Ty Nant Pony and Llanfihangel Pony Paths to Cadair Idris, the Precipice, Torrent and Glyn Aran Walks near Dolgellau, and Branwen's Walk near Harlech.

The Forestry Commission has numerous waymarked trails. There are waymarked walks varying in length from 1.5 to 3 km (1–2 miles) in the Newborough Forest on Anglesey.

For the Gwydyr Forest near Betws-y-Coed the Commission publishes two walk-packs, each containing six walks. Walks 1–6 are close to Betws, and vary in length from 2.5 to 5.5 km (1½–3½ miles). Walks 7–12 move further afield and vary from 2.5 to 10.5 km (1½–6½ miles). Leaflets are available from the National Park's Y Stablau Visitors Centre, Betws-y-Coed.

There are two waymarked trails, of 3 and 5 km (2 and 3 miles in the Beddgelert Forest.

There are several trails, from 1 to 4.5 km (½–2¾ miles) starting from the Bod Petrual Visitors Centre in the Clocaenog Forest, while those in the Moel Famau Forest to the north-east vary from 3 to 8 km (2–5 miles).

Finally the Coed-y-Brenin Forest is criss-crossed by paths, and the Eden Valley Trail extends for 1.25 km (¾ mile) from the

Maesgwm Visitors Centre, from where trail leaflets are available.

Waymarked trails, both woodland and industrial, also exist in the Padarn Country Park, Llanberis.

Walks for the Disabled
From the A5 at Miner's Bridge, at the western end of Betws-y-Coed, the Garth Falls Walk is a smooth paved trail with handrails. Descriptive labels at intervals along the walk are repeated in braille. A leaflet on the walk is available from the Y Stablau Visitors Centre, Betws-y-Coed.

The Penmaenpool to Morfa Mawddach Walk runs for 8 km (5 miles) along the southern shore of the Mawddach estuary. The walk is along a disused railway track through fine country renowned for its bird life. The western end of the walk has been surfaced for wheelchairs over a distance of about 500 m though, since the remainder of the walk is flat and even, many visitors may be able to continue further. The walk has a continuous wooden hand-rail with bilingual braille labels to warn of seats that are placed at regular intervals.

APPENDIX 2 TRANSPORT AND WEATHER

The National Park Visitors Centres have copies of a 'bus and train' map of Gwynedd that shows all routes, with the bus routes given their appropriate Gwynedd Bus Number. The centre will also supply timetables for the routes.

Many of the services are infrequent, and have either a limited or no service on Sundays and holidays, but may be convenient for 'one-off' trips. An exception is the Snowdon Sherpa bus, most specifically the half-hourly service that runs daily from mid-July to early September from Llanberis to Pen-y-Gwryd, and is invaluable for ascents starting from Pen-y-Pass. Sadly the same fine service is not available in the Ogwen valley, which is poorly served – though, in fairness, parking is a little easier there. The Sherpa also runs down the western side of Snowdon (Caernarfon-Rhyd Ddu-Beddgelert) and links Llanrwst to Porthmadog via

Betws-y-Coed, Capel Curig, Pen-y-Gwryd and Beddgelert. It also
runs from Caernarfon to Llanberis, and from Llandudno to
Llanberis, via Llanrwst, Betws-y-Coed, Capel Curig and
Pen-y-Gwryd.

Weather Reports
A daily weather forecast is available for the whole National Park by
ringing Llanberis (0286) 870120.

   More specific forecasts are posted daily at the Gorphywsfa Café,
and are also available at the Plas-y-Brenin and Ogwen Cottage
Mountain Centres.

APPENDIX 3 USEFUL ADDRESSES

Snowdonia National Park

Snowdonia National Park Authority
National Park Office
Penrhyndeudraeth
Gwynedd LL48 6LS
Tel: Penrhyndeudraeth (0766) 770274

National Park Study Centre
Plas Tan-y-Bwlch
Maentwrog
Blaenau Ffestiniog
Gwynedd LL41 3YU
Tel: (0766) 85324

Youth and Schools Liaison Service
Tel: (0766) 770274

Information Centres

Aberdyfi	Tel: (0654) 472321
Bala	(0678) 520367
Betws-y-Coed	(06902) 665

Blaenau Ffestiniog	(0766) 830360
Dolgellau	(0341) 422888
Harlech	(0766) 780658
Llanberis	(0286) 870636

Conservation Organisations

Council for National Parks
45 Shelton Street
London WC2H 9HJ
Tel: (01) 240 3603

Countryside Commission
John Dower House
Crescent Place
Cheltenham
Glos GL50 3RA
Tel: (0242) 21381

Countryside Commission Office for Wales
Ladywell House
Newtown
Powys SY16 1RD
Tel: (0686) 26799

Nature Conservancy Council (for Permits)
Penrhos Road
Bangor
Tel: (0248) 355141

The National Trust
36 Queen Anne's Gate
London SW1H 9AS
Tel: (01) 222 9251

The National Trust
Trinity Square
Llandudno
Tel (0492) 74421

Snowdonia National Park Society
Capel Curig
Tel: (06904) 234

General

Forestry Commission
Gwydr Uchaf
Llanrwst
Tel: (0492) 640578

North Wales Tourism Council
77 Conwy Road
Colwyn Bay
Clwyd
Tel: (0492) 31731

Index